La Indianidad

The Indigenous World Before Latin Americans

The Indigenous World
Before Latin Americans

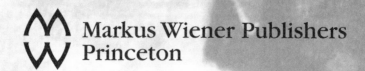

Markus Wiener Publishers
Princeton

La Indianidad

HERNÁN HORNA

Introduction by Jane M. Rausch

For information write to:
Markus Wiener Publishers
231 Nassau Street, Princeton, NJ 08542

Book design by Cheryl Mirkin
Cover design by Maria Madonna Davidoff
The painting on pp. ii–iii is by Roy Z. Chamlee.

Library of Congress Cataloging-in-Publication Data

Horna, Hernán.
[Indianidad antes de la independencia latinoamericana. English]
La Indianidad=The indigenous world before Latin Americans/by Hernán Horna;
    Introduction by Jane Rausch.
    Includes bibliographical references and index.
    ISBN 1-55876-268-x (hc)
    ISBN 1-55876-269-8 (pbk)
    1. Indians—History 2. Indians—Ethnic identity.
    3. indians, Treatment of—Latin America. 4. Latin America—Race relations.
    5. Latin America—Politics and government.
    I. Title: Indigenous world before Latin Americans. II. Title.
    E65.H69313 2001
    323.1'198—dc21   2001026979

Printed in the United States of America on acid-free paper.

CONTENTS

Acknowledgments   vii

Introduction by Jane M. Rausch   ix

Toward a History of the Amerindian Civilizations   1
   Another Historical Perspective   3
   The First Emigrants   8
   Agriculture   11
   Foreign Contacts   17
   Diffusionism versus Isolationism   29
   Religious Fanaticism   31
   Human Sacrifice   33
   The Mayas   36
   The Aztecs   46
   The Incas   56

From Colonization to Decolonization   79
   The Conquest Revisited   81
   From Underdevelopment to Neocolonialism   109

Notes   153

Bibliography   167

Index   177

The bibliography included in this book has been cited and consulted for its elaboration. The author has benefited directly and indirectly from other works, conversations, and dialogues with colleagues and friends as well as the Latin American Seminars at Uppsala University. The present effort has attempted to reconstruct an Amerindian history without bypassing the traditional historiography about Latin America. Among the intellectuals who have given me the greatest help are Jane M. Rausch and Harald Runblom. Their constructive critique and encouragement were present from the outset of my project. Carlos Arroyo, Håkan Bengtsson, Roy Z. Chamlee, Jr., Melquiades Horna, Åke Hultkrantz, Lillemor Ingvaldsson, Saturo Kumano, José Del Carmen Marín, José Matos Mar, Magnus Mörner, Robin Oakely, Eva Österberg, Cynthia Radding, Myrna Rennison, Rolf Torstendahl and Anita R. Wahlgren have also read and made commentaries to more primitive versions of my work. They have greatly contributed to improving the quality of this book. However, this author alone is responsible for the expressed perspectives, text citations, or any mistake. Special thanks are extended to David Muñoz for his assistance in the reproduction and compilation of the illustrations.

Hernán Horna
Uppsala, Sweden

Of the many new approaches that Latin American historians have been exploring in the last twenty years, certainly none is more important than their reassessment of the development of Native American civilizations before the arrival of the Spanish and Portuguese, during the three hundred years of European colonization, and after the declaration of independent nation-states. This new path has not been an easy one because over the centuries many native artifacts have been destroyed and their memories suppressed. To arrive at an authentic ethnohistory of Amerindians and to understand the multi-dimensional nature of the ancient indigenous world, historians must rely upon the work of archaeologists, anthropologists, as well as linguists— investigations that are constantly being amended as new discoveries are announced. They must also reexamine Spanish and Portuguese texts written in the early years of conquest and settlement to uncover the Indian voices that lie beneath the surface of documents written from an essentially Eurocentric point of view. Despite these difficulties, new evidence has been emerging that challenges the traditionally-held notion that native Americans were "noble savages" living in an Eden-like paradise, or conversely, that they were isolated, primitive people, quickly defeated by "superior" Europeans who then proceeded to provide them with the technological and cultural developments of a "higher civilization." The major contribution of *La Indianidad: The Indigenous World Before Latin Americans* by Dr. Hernán Horna is to integrate these new insights into a concise indigenous history, which, without bypassing western historiography, covers not only the nature of the Amerindian world before the arrival of Columbus, but also their post-conquest adaptations, co-existence and struggle against colonial rule and subjugation by the Catholic Church and state.

It may seem surprising that a historian working in an isolated Swedish University would become the first to produce such a history of indigenous Latin America, but Dr. Horna is uniquely qualified for this task. Born in Cajamarca, Peru in 1942, he moved to the United States at the age of eighteen where in due course he received his B.A. from Belmont College in Nashville, Tennessee and his M.A. from Middle Tennessee State University in 1966. Horna began teaching at Western Illinois University while completing his Ph.D. at Vanderbilt University where, under the guidance of Dr. J. León Helguera, his attention was directed to the colorful saga of railroad building in Colombia. His dissertation, finished in 1970, was later to become a book, *Transport Modernization and Entrepreneurship in Nineteenth Century Colombia: Cisneros & Friends* (Uppsala, Sweden, 1992), and it remains the most thorough study of this aspect of nineteenth-century Colombian development. After he met Swedish-born Anita Wahlgren, who was to become his wife, Horna moved to Sweden where he secured an appointment as Docent in the History Department of Uppsala University. There, for twenty-three years he has taught a variety of courses on Latin America and published essays in Swedish, English, and Colombian journals on ancient America and Asiatic contacts with ancient America. It is perhaps this fortuitous opportunity of working outside the Western Hemisphere, along with his trips to the Far East as a visiting professor in China and Japan, that explains Horna's ability to take a fresh, and one might even say "iconoclastic," look at the history of the New World.

And *La Indianidad* is nothing if not iconoclastic. To achieve his goal to counter stereotypes of Indians as "victims, pagans, inferior, and irrational," Horna, from the first chapter, challenges traditional views of Amerindian civilizations by suggesting that pre-Columbian migration into the Western Hemisphere may have come by way of Antarctica, Melanesia and Australia as well as from Asia via what is now the Bering Sea. While granting that the various civilizations developed for the most part autochthonously, he convincingly builds a case for numerous interactions between the New World peoples themselves and with Scandinavians, Africans, and especially Asians. To emphasize that Amerindians were no less creative than any other so-called "race," he demonstrates that the Incas as well as the Mayas had a system of writing, and notes that, by modern standards, the widely cited Indian practices of human sacrifices and cannibalism were no more irrational or cruel than the execution of almost half a million Europeans accused of witchcraft from the fifteenth to the seventeenth centuries.

Horna shows that the Incas' ability to care for their widespread and populous empire has not been duplicated since the Spanish conquest, suggesting that Amerindian technology, efficiency and productivity surpassed that achieved by Western Europe. "The history of the Amerindians," he contends, "does not end with the arrival of Western civilization." Despite being subjugated, oppressed and repressed, by the outset of the third millennium Amerindians exist in numbers similar to those at the time of Columbus even though, due to assimilation, in many countries they remain a minority of the Latin American population. Nevertheless, "the essence of ancient dreams has survived," and Horna's book provides a context for understanding the resilience of native languages, cultures and populations throughout the nineteenth and twentieth century as well as the demands their leaders are now making for recognition and justice in lands stretching from Patagonia to Alaska.

Not every Latin Americanist will accept all of Dr. Horna's assertions, but the evidence he has marshaled to back up his conclusions requires that his ideas be given serious consideration. At the very least, I believe that *La Indianiadad* will serve as a starting point for some very stimulating scholarly debates.

Jane M. Rausch
University of Massachusetts—Amherst

Toward a History of the Amerindian Civilizations

There are two separate histories of the Americas: that of Indian America and that of Americans under the influence of Western civilization. Until recently, Indians have been regarded as savages without history, but in reality this meant only that their history was unknown. Whites created a vision of the New World and gradually imposed it on the natives. Not independent of this has been some variety of European xenophobia toward non-Whites. Of course, it is now clear that so-called scientific theories of racial superiority have no validity.

Our knowledge of events before Christopher Columbus is quite sparse, not only because historiography has been Eurocentric, but because practitioners of the historical discipline have been reluctant to accept the comparative perspectives of the social sciences. Experience has demonstrated, however, that the story of a defeated people is not the monopoly of any particular discipline or the sole property of historians. Fortunately, in our age of awareness there has been greater concern for understanding the world beyond the West. Not independent of this preoccupation is the presence in several Western countries of ethnic minorities that are often the victims of discrimination. An inquisitive trend is developing in many quarters of the West toward comprehending the material and mental cultures of the underdog. For example, several U.S. researchers, in an effort to understand Afro-American slavery in their own history, are producing comparative studies of slavery in other parts of the world. The rise of so-called ethnohistory has become a common concern of historians, anthropologists, and archeologists.

Since most of the native writings, and the graphic symbols that expressed Indian science and culture, have been destroyed, we have learned about Amerindian accomplishments mostly through the eyes of the victorious Western civilization. The three or four pre-Columbian Mayan manuscripts that remain, as well as their stone glyphs, still have not been fully translated. An understanding of the defeated requires that modern scholars take an interdisciplinary approach. Even a cross-cultural comparative perspective is most welcome; since ancient America constituted at first an Asian migration frontier, comparative perspectives from the point of view of the old Asian civilizations, using Asian categories and rationalities, are necessary. One can maintain that if either China or Japan had conquered the Americas, the so-called primitivism and *mentalité* of American Indians would be less bewildering. It is now clear that pre-Columbian Indian history does not represent those early stages of human development that the first European anthropologists attempted to find in their scientific studies of the "Red Man."[1]

Western historiography has not yet overcome its original paternalistic perception of the Conquista (conquest) as a confrontation between two peoples in which the victorious Europeans have been presented as a Christian—and superior—race, and therefore more civilized. The defeated were pagan, inferior, and thus primitive or irrational. Even the magnanimous "protector of Indians," Father Bartolomé de Las Casas (1474–1566), was heir to the racist European culture that "discovered" and conquered America. That Las Casas was not completely free from Aristotelian values is shown by his paternalistic view of the conquered society: He favored Black slavery, in order to mitigate the abusive labor requirements imposed on the Amerindians. In his opinion, Indians were more rational than Blacks: "They had nothing to hinder them from enjoying heaven, but their ignorance of the true God."[2] In reality, Las Casas was seeking an exclusive and paternalistic control of the Indians by the Catholic Church.[3] Colonial priests and monks would eventually accept the idea that Indians could be rational enough to be Christians, but not rational enough to become prelates.[4]

During the sixteenth and seventeenth centuries, a number of Indians and Mestizos from the Andes and Mesoamerica (the area between, and including, Mexico and Costa Rica) had learned Spanish and were able to write about some intimate aspects of their culture and the events that brought about its cataclysmic collapse. But these authors, like the Whites, wrote within the limitations imposed by the new colonialist order. The native authors had been trained, manipulated, and selected by the Christian clergy. The studies sponsored by the clergy and by the colonial state were biased, and generally dealt only with the subjects about which the sponsors wished to prove a point. Native authors had to practice self-censorship or contend with the official censorship of the church, the Inquisition, and the state; they had to maintain a strictly antipagan attitude. The practical consequence of this censorship is that what is presented as history is in reality only the skewed version of events as written by the colonialists. Eventually the Catholic Church bureaucracy decided to abandon the high-quality education of chosen natives. The Indianist writings authored by Indians and Mestizos of the so-called golden sixteenth century gradually disappeared when Indian children were no longer properly educated. The colonial state and the church united, formally and informally, in the subjugation of the defeated cultures. Furthermore, these censored and diluted accounts of the Indian past were either prohibited or restricted after the Indian revolts of the late eighteenth century. The limitations on what was written about Indians makes it imperative that we read between the lines in order to obtain a more accurate view of these defeated people.

The Latin American independence movement was led by *criollos* (white elites), who would be the real inheritors of Iberian power. The idea of democracy, among the most progressive local elites of the nineteenth century, was derived from the ideals and slogans of European liberalism. Such an approach, which was further aggravated by the advent of positivism and social Darwinism, led to the abandonment of Indian rights. International racism was not officially defeated until the downfall of Nazi Germany, but it is clear that racism still has not been eradicated either locally or in a larger dimension. It was not until the middle of the twentieth century that the terms "developing" or "underdeveloped" were invented to replace the notion of "uncivilized nations."

The *indigenista* movement, the intellectual trend that urged a revival of Indian culture in countries with large Indian populations, did not take place until the turn of the twentieth century. In Peru, it was the result of a crisis of identity among Peruvian intellectuals, caused by the defeat in the war against Chile (1879–1883). The more virulent Mexican *indigenismo* sprang from the revolution of 1911. Unfortunately, the indigenista movement was misunderstood and attacked by Hispanistas, both Spanish and Spanish Americans, who portrayed the efforts of the indigenistas as the revival of the Black Legend and the vilification of Spanish colonial rule.[5] But as the American historian Charles Gibson has correctly noted, "any student . . . could find in the colonial archives of Spain and Spanish America far more evidence than the one provided by Las Casas" in his criticism of Spanish colonialism.[6] Regardless of whether Spain was a humane or a tyrannical colonial power, the history of the vanquished Indians has to recognize them, first of all, as the oppressed victims of colonialism. None of the European nations fought and colonized the Amerindians for humanitarian reasons.

Just as Amerindian historiography requires an interdisciplinary perspective, many Indian political activists argue vigorously that their history cannot be written solely by professional historians. So much has been neglected or disdained for such a long time that the academic disciplines need the help of political activists and those active in the area of Indian history. The results of these joint efforts must then be brought under the scrutiny not only of historians, but of average citizens of the modern world, who are still bombarded with negative stereotypes reflected and generated by cowboy movies, comic strips, and other mass media outlets.

In pursuit of this goal, several Indian political organizations in the United States, Latin America, and Canada have already invested some of their meager resources in the movie industry. The immediate outcome has been the appearance of popular films with Indian perspectives. The Peruvian film *Where the Condors are Born*, and the America cowboy thriller with Dustin Hoffman, *Little Big Man*, were financed by the new and emerging Amerindian activism. The films by the Guatemalan movie director Felix Zurita, as well as those of the

Bolivian Jorge Sanjinés, the Ecuadorian Alberto Muenala, and the Peruvians César Galindo and Federico García Hurtado, reflect efforts to present an Indian perspective. The use of cybernetic technology and amateur Indian articulators, in order to illustrate the indigenous world, by the American artist and producer Kevin Costner is a notable advance that augurs new efforts for the Indian cause. But Amerindians still struggle against discrimination by and exclusion from the modernized world.

THE FIRST EMIGRANTS

Until recently it was maintained that the Indians migrated from Asia by way of the Bering Straits, at a Paleolithic level of culture, sometime between the years 20,000 and 10,000 B.C.E. However, recent archeological discoveries and new methods of dating, especially the use of carbon 14, and a greater sophistication in the practice of stratigraphy, have pushed back the period of migration to roughly between forty and eighty thousand years B.C.E. Furthermore, it is now accepted that not all the migrants could have come during the same period.[7]

The anthropologists Paul Rivet and A. A. Mendes Correa have also maintained that some of the ancient Amerindians could have come across Antarctica in a northward direction. The so-called French School initiated by Rivet and his students and followers has a greater degree of acceptance among Latin American academic circles. Although the French School accepts the Asian migration through the Bering Straits as the fundamental migratory route, it maintains that people from Melanesia and Australia migrated concurrently to America by way of Antarctica. Such an affirmation is based on anthropological, ethnological, and linguistic similarities among the inhabitants of Melanesia and Australia and the American Indians. Rivet has noted the Melanesian presence extending from Lower California and the American West to Colombia, Ecuador, Peru, Brazil, and Argentina. According to the Portuguese anthropologist Mendes Correa, the Australian influence is more strikingly apparent among the Indians from Patagonia and Tierra del Fuego.[8] In any case, both migration theories depend on changes in climate and in oceanic water levels in the

Arctic and Antarctic for their validity.[9] Theories about the autochthonous origin of the Amerindians, however, were overruled when the skeletons and bones presented as evidence were declared to be of more recent age with the help of carbon 14.[10]

The theory proclaiming a migration from Asia to the New World through the Bering Strait has had the most international scholarly support, and it is often the only one mentioned in school texts. If we accept the validity of this proposition, it establishes that twenty thousand years before the Christian era, the Asiatic migration stopped, and that five thousand years later the migrants had reached the southernmost end of the Western Hemisphere. The most ancient murals of the Americas are found in the Amazon jungle and are dated to fourteen thousand years ago.[11] Nevertheless, the migratory process within the American continent continued until the discovery or creation of a more secure source of nutrition. This theory has gained the greatest acceptance, and very soon it may be accepted as irrefutable fact—unless, of course, further research proves otherwise.

Four major human groups are said to have migrated through the Bering Strait: Australians, Asians (Mongols), Uralic peoples, and Malayan-Polynesians. Thus, the Eskimos would descend from the Mongols, the North American Indians from Uralic peoples, and the Latin American Indians from a mixture of Malayan-Polynesians with other Asian groups. These theories are based on the analysis of blood types, linguistic similarities, and physical appearance, including the so-called Mongolian Spot, which is a mark the size of a medium-sized coin that appears on the buttocks of Mongolian children and generally disappears before adolescence. The Mongolian Spot has been observed in the majority of Indian children from Latin America as well as among the Eskimos.

All the emigrants from Asia must have come before the so-called agricultural revolution and at the end of the Paleolithic period. They would have been hunters who followed their prey, and without the distinctive characteristics of later Asiatic cultures. In other words, they depended on Mother Nature for their survival. Later on, the first migrants learned to understand and benefit regularly from the local ecology. It was a situation similar to that of Europe before the

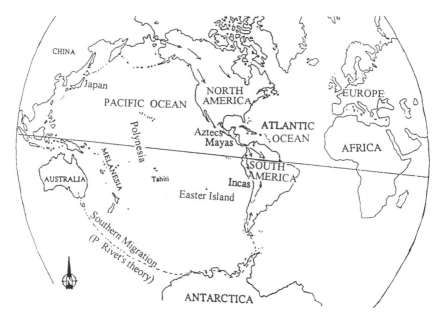

Migratory routes from Asia to the New World.

Renaissance, when the culture was based on living in harmony with nature. It is germane to note that such an indigenous way of life still prevails in its purest form in the more isolated regions of the Amazon jungle.

As archeologists, anthropologists, and ethnologists became interested in the Americas as a field of research, the theories of ethnoracial, linguistic, and cultural homogeneity were critically appraised. It was noted, for example, that Indians were phenotypically varied and linguistically complex, with more than twelve hundred different dialects stemming from 140 different linguistic stocks. There were twenty-two distinct cultural areas in the pre-Columbian Americas. Many physical and cultural differences distinguished the Indian tribes, especially between North and South America, but the pre-Hispanic inhabitants were more linked by their many-faceted similarities than they were separated by their differences. Certainly, pre-Columbian Amerindians represented the human crystallization of peoples that had intermingled with each other and had shared the New World for thousands of years.

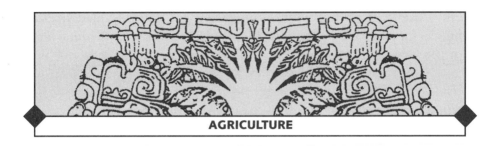

AGRICULTURE

In the New World, as in the Old, it has been difficult to establish where agriculture originated, but it is accepted that about ten thousand years ago the method for the acquisition of food began to change gradually, as humans made the transition from food gatherers to cultivators and producers of foods. Apparently, agriculture began to be practiced simultaneously and independently in different places. The wild grains that probably were the predecessors of cereal crops have been found in several places. In the Americas, maize (Indian corn) was the only cereal, but Indians cultivated many other products: peanuts, beans, squash, papayas, guavas, avocados, pineapples, tomatoes, chili peppers, pumpkins, potatoes, sweet potatoes, yucca, cacao, tobacco, and the best cotton in the world.[12] The cultivation of tubers and poisonous plants became an Amerindian specialty. The inhabitants of tropical America were the first to make good use of the manioc; from its roots they extracted food, alcoholic beverages, and poison for hunting. Through carbon 14 it has been established that the chickpeas and beans found in Thailand date from 7000 years B.C.E.; wheat and barley in Iraq from 6750 B.C.E.; beans in Peru from 6000 B.C.E.; squash, melons, and maize in Mexico from 7000 to 5000 B.C.E.[13] Amerindians domesticated more than a hundred plants, which is the equivalent of the total vegetable domestication in Eurasia, from Morocco to Kamchatka and from Norway to Malaya. More than fifty percent of all the agricultural products of the United States originate from Amerindian cultivation.[14]

As humans made the transition from food-gatherers to cultivators, they simultaneously learned to domesticate animals. Dogs, horses, cows, donkeys, goats, sheep, and pigs became more permanent human companions as well as nutrition sources in the Old World, while in the New World the Amerindians developed a similar relationship with llamas, alpacas, vicuñas, guinea pigs, turkeys, iguanas, and small hairless dogs. Unfortunately, Amerindians did not have access to draft animals like horses or donkeys. Llamas, the strongest of the American domesticated animals, cannot be loaded with much more than fifty pounds. Despite all assertions about the Amerindian incapacity to conceive the mechanical wheel, they did indeed know its operative principles: Toys with four wheels in a vehicular configuration were excavated in Mesoamerica and the Andes soon after World War II. It has also been asserted that the Incas transported the gigantic stones for their monuments and architectural constructions with the help of rollers. The French-Bulgarian philosopher Tzvetan Todorov has perceptively noted that for the Mayas, the graphic and mental image of time was the wheel.[15] But it can be said that the wheel of pre-Columbian America still did not have the functionality that it had in the Old World. The vehicular wheel for the Amerindians played a role something like that of gunpowder for the ancient Chinese.

The advent of agriculture constituted a radical change that transformed all facets of life among ancient humans. Men and women left their nomadic life and began the civilizing process of building houses, towns, and systems of irrigation. Perhaps the most notorious characteristic of Neolithic culture was the creation of institutions. An institution can be defined as the combination of beliefs and activities organized for the satisfaction of a group's needs. Among the oldest institutions are the family, religion, and, later, the state. The origin of the state in antiquity was doubtless the result of numerous factors, but one of the most important was indeed agriculture. The change in the mode of procuring food brought an increase in production, which in turn intensified the confrontation of individual and group interests. Under those new conditions, old traditions and customs could not be sufficient to define the rights and obligations of the members of society. New measures of social control became necessary, facilitating the establishment of sovereign governments controlled by mystics and shamans, who could exercise coercive authority and dominate their compatriots. In fact, it is not difficult to verify that in pre-Columbian America, the highest levels of social organization were found in regions where large populations lived by the cultivation of small fertile areas.

The absence of heavy draft animals such as horses in the Americas caused these agricultural societies to derive a greater amount of productive energy from the intensification and organization of human labor. Such circumstances encouraged, in Mesoamerica and the Andes, as well as in China and the Middle East, the development of the state in its most sophisticated expression in antiquity. State formation in ancient America has been analyzed from both a liberal and a Marxist perspective: The former proclaims that the state is at the service of the entire society, while Marxist historical materialism maintains that the dominant classes benefit most from such an institution. That the pre-Columbian state existed, and was real, can be verified regardless of the ideology used to analyze it.[16]

By approximately the year 1500 B.C.E., we observe, in many parts of the Americas, the development of simple farming, combined with food gathering, fishing, hunting, and beekeeping. The use of stone tools and weaving is evident. Archeological research is now revealing that, while farming developed even earlier in several places in the Americas, the combination of agriculture and cattle-breeding was basically a phenomenon of the Old World, except in the case of the ancient Peruvians, who had llamas. With the growth of agriculture, the worship of Pachamama (sacred Mother Earth)[17] became one of the most deeply rooted religious practices among the neophyte Amerindian farmers. The main centers of cultural diffusion were the central Andes and Mesoamerica, where advanced cultural and technological developments place the Indians at nearly the same level of development as the other contemporary centers of world civilization.

The Amerindian population at the time when Columbus "discovered" America has been calculated at between fourteen and one hundred million.[18] More recent calculations and research tend to support the latter figure, but this author accepts the more modest view proposed by the Spanish historian Guillermo Céspedes, who estimates

Pre-Columbian toys with wheels.

the population at about eighty million.[19] From such an affirmation it
can be deduced that the great majority of the Amerindians belonged
to the high cultures.[20] It must be conceded that our knowledge about
the less developed cultures is very precarious. One of the most difficult problems in the study of those cultures has been the absence of
archeological remains and ethnographic sources. It can be said that
the great majority of those cultures practiced several kinds of rustic
agriculture in which women played an important and often dominant
role. The majority of the human groups in that developmental stage
maintained a sedentary life with complex cultural and social characteristics, but they did not develop urban centers in the real meaning
of the word. However, recent research has revealed, for example, that
the Mississippi culture traded through river networks with one third
of the North American continent, and that its capital, Sun City (now
Cahokia, Illinois), had more than forty thousand inhabitants in the
thirteenth century.[21]

The low, like the high cultures, lived in a moral world in which
they tried to adapt their lives to their perception of nature's laws.
Their observations of nature affected their religious beliefs and moral
laws, and also taught them botanical and ecological concepts. It
should surprise no one that their medical knowledge has survived up
to the beginning of the third millennium, and that many pharmaceutical companies still learn and profit from their supposedly primitive

knowledge of plants. The Amerindian knowledge of the geology allowed them to utilize the subterranean water currents. In the high cultures, irrigation channels and water fountains (*cenotes, huachaques, puquios*) functioned in an integrated system.

Despite the fact that the less developed cultures had contacts with the high civilizations, they themselves did not depart from their nearly absolute disuse of metal implements and other artifacts enjoyed by the more "civilized" Indians. The similarity of cultural elements among the Amerindians, however, as well as the discovery of archeological remains and other products away from their places of origin,[22] suggests that the history of the advanced and less advanced Amerindians cannot be written separately and without interrelation.

Unfortunately, one of the most neglected areas of archeological research has been the interrelations among the different Amerindian cultures. It is germane to remember that the mountains and distances never were absolute barriers. There is not any region in the American continent where signs of isolated development can be found. We know that where there were Indians with gold, the Spanish found them, but the Spanish "discovered" them because the Indians were their guides. It has been easier for scholars to accept the idea that the Amerindians migrated from Asia and colonized the whole area, thousands of years ago in an almost subhuman condition, than for them to admit the existence of contacts among Indians at the time when the Spanish arrived. Such an attitude reflects, at the very least, intellectual short-sightedness. To the contrary, there were contacts by land and sea. Finding a Mexican Marco Polo who visited the Andes is, of course, asking too much, but the Incas had names, such as Capac Cochas, for peoples who came from distant places by sea.[23]

The reasons for the varying levels of development among the Amerindians have constituted a conundrum whose proposed solutions border on mysticism. The experts have proposed geographic, climatic, ecological, cultural, and socioeconomic explanatory factors, but as with the contemporary debate about industrialized and developing or underdeveloped nations, they have not reached a consensus. Apparently, the answer to this eternal and enduring problem can be viewed in many ways, and it is from that perspective that research must be conducted. The history of humankind has demonstrated that economic development is not a homogeneous process. Indeed, the most significant aspect of the lives of the pre-Columbian Amerindians was their relationship to Mother Earth and nature, and it was that relationship that determined the use of their physical and mental capacities.

FOREIGN CONTACTS

In view of the fact that it is not impossible for humans to swim from Europe to Africa, as well as to walk to Asia, it must be conceded that the most remarkable aspect of the ancient American civilizations was their isolated and independent growth: the reality of this cannot be overemphasized. Nevertheless, Americanist researchers continue to discover evidence of outside influences, such as Negroid people in Mesoamerica;[24] Polynesian-style artifacts, sculptures, and other cultural links in Peru and northern Chile; and pottery of ancient Japanese style (Jomon) in Ecuador.[25] Likewise, the similarities in the iconography of Central Asia and North America are very noticeable.[26] Eastern Mediterranean inscriptions have also been identified in several parts of the continent.[27]

It is now accepted that the Scandinavians maintained small colonies along the northeastern coast of the North American continent from the tenth to the fifteenth centuries, but without realizing that they had discovered the New World. Apparently this meager colonization did not produce cultural diffusion or the introduction of horses.[28] The astonishing similarities between art styles of Amerindian and oriental civilizations suggest transpacific contact at the time of the high cultures.[29] Western scholars have noted artistic and architectural similarities between the Peruvian Chavín culture and China of the Chang Dynasty (1200–1100 B.C.E.). Similar links to the Orient have been found among the pre-Inca Mochica Indians of the northern Peruvian coast. Moreover, the Chimu tribe, which founded its capital city of Chan Chan, near Trujillo, and dominated the Mochicas until shortly before the Spanish invasion, traced their ancestry to naviga-

Sea currents of the Pacific that could have facilitated contacts
between Asia and pre-Columbian America.

tors who came in boats from the Pacific.[30]

In the realistic Mochica ceramics, distinctive oriental faces with
mustaches, goatees, and other beards can be found. Negroids, or
Australoids, are also represented in Mochica pottery (*huacos*).[31] In
the Nazca ceramics of coastal Peru, Chinese letters and phrases have
been discovered.[32] Chan Chan and other Chimu cities are also entire-

Dragon in Mochica ceramic.

ly different from other pre-
Columbian cities; they had the
same styles, structures, and
designs as those of China during the seventh and ninth centuries C.E.[33] Chan Chan has the
unique distinction of having a
Huaca (holy place) in honor of
the dragon. The cult of the dragon, or serpent with arms, is of
Asian origin,[34] and had even

Dragon huaca in Chan Chan (Peru).

extended itself to Europe, before the rise of Christianity eliminated it as a form of devil worship. In China, the dragon was the deity of earthquakes and storms. The dragon changed its physical appearance according to the local ecology and fauna. Despite its fearsome appearance and dangerous characteristics, this mythological animal had a protective role. In other words, the positive and the negative could be found inside the same entity, expressing the duality of life. The American ethnohistorian R. C. Padden, in his study of the Aztec spiritual world, concludes that it has an astonishing "similarity with the Yang and Yin of China."[35] Likewise, the Mexican anthropologist Miguel León-Portilla perceives a similarity between Mesoamerican literature and that of Asia. He further notes that some of its concepts, violent metaphors, and rhythmic parallelism of phrases remind us of the invocations and hymns of the Hindu writings in the Rig Veda.[36]

The great chronicler of the Mexican conquest, Bernal Díaz del Castillo, informs us that in the Aztec temples there were dragons as big as bulls.[37] What some Westerners called "devilish serpents," which the Indians were said to revere, were indeed dragons.[38] The deities that came and went by the seas, Viracocha, Quetzalcoatl, and Kukul-Chan, were represented by serpents and dragons. The ethnohistorical evidence clearly indicates that the first Viracochas came from Asia rather than Europe.

According to the Spanish *cronistas* (chroniclers), the Inca emperor Tupac Yupanqui (1471–1493) led more than twenty thousand Peruvians in balsa rafts on an expedition for approximately a year to what some modern scholars have taken to be Polynesia and Melanesia. Among the booty captured or traded by the Incan expedition were several Negroid or Australoid people, some of whom were kept alive in Cuzco until the Spanish arrival.[39] Spanish cronistas also reported that when Vasco Núñez de Balboa arrived at Panama, he noticed that several Indian chiefs had slaves of Negroid appearance.[40] The anthropological, cultural, linguistic, and other similarities between the Indians of western South America and Polynesia and Melanesia cannot be ignored. Even though the Inca Empire had its most splendid development in the Andean highlands, the coastal inhabitants were excellent fishermen and sailors.[41] Indeed, the history of the Pacific islands and that of the pre-European American continent are not entirely separate. For example, architectonic buildings of Asiatic and Andean styles have been found on Easter Island.[42]

On his first journey to America, Columbus's experts informed him that they had seen an Indian woman wearing on her nose a metallic coin with Chinese letters.[43] The only place where copper and tin coins were used in pre-European America was in the Pacific Mesoamerican coast.[44] When Columbus tried for the first time to conquer the American mainland in Ver-Aguas (the present Panama Canal Zone), the natives informed him not only that on the other side existed a sea, but also that by such a route he could reach China. In Ver-Aguas, Columbus found stucco walls that he and his experts supposed to be of Chinese origin. Unfortunately, the ship loaded with the stucco remains sank when the conquering expedition failed.[45] Columbus was not mistaken in supposing that he might have reached China by traveling west; he just miscalculated the distances.

Ancient Chinese scholars wrote extensively of lands beyond what they called the Great Eastern Sea. The oldest document describing what could be the Western Hemisphere dates back to the second century B.C.E. and is known as the *Chu-chu-i* (History of Ten Islands). One of those islands was called Fusang for its abundance in magical plants. Until very recently, Western scholars asserted that Fusang was Japan; however, new research in China has definitely concluded that it was not. For example, a recently excavated granite map from the eleventh century C.E. clearly includes the islands of both Japan and Fusang. Likewise, in the ancient Chinese magic literature such as the *Shan Hai Jing* (Classic of Mountains and Seas), it is written that on the other side of the Great Eastern Sea there is a continent. In this work there are descriptions of geography and fauna that are found in North America and the Aleutian Islands.

Subsequent documentation about Fusang dates from the sixth century C.E. In the history of the Liang Dynasty, it is written that during the Buddhist exile of Fasien, Hui Chan, a Chinese monk from Kashmir, visited Fusang with his followers for forty years. This expedition came to America via the Kurishivo current, landing in Mesoamerica. It continued afterward to the western South American coast, and then returned to Asia by the South Pacific. In the returning cargo, Hui Chan carried the equivalent of 150 kilograms of a special "silk" to be presented to the Son of Heaven. One of the most interesting aspects of Hui Chan's story is that its narrative was written and archived in the imperial library. The descriptions of Fusang are more reminiscent of pre-Columbian Mexico than of any other part of the Americas. However, in the tradition of the Chinese sagas, the narratives also contain descriptions of other places.

The journey of Hui Chan must be understood in the context of China's historical presence in the Pacific archipelago. During the period in which Hui Chan "rediscovered" Fusang, many Chinese expeditions explored the Pacific Ocean in search of magic plants that would guarantee eternal youth. These expeditions were searching not for commercial routes, but rather for unusual things like medicines and the wool of "sea sheep." Chinese historians now maintain not only that the Chinese discovered America, but that China had sporadic contacts with the Americas until shortly before Columbus's arrival. The great controversy in Chinese historiography is not about whether the Chinese discovered America, but rather about which parts of America they discovered.[46]

Western researchers have recently acknowledged that Chinese maritime technology was more advanced than that of Europe before Columbus.[47] In the Cantonese shipyards, vessels of four masts and one hundred tons were already being built during the second century C.E. Such ships made journeys of more than twelve months in the high seas. Possibly from the middle of the ninth century, Chinese ships were equipped with magnetic compasses. It has also been proven that between 1403 and 1419, Chinese ships of up to one hundred meters in length and fifteen hundred tons were built, and that those vessels were especially designed for long ocean voyages.[48]

With the death of the Chinese emperor Yong-le, in 1423, state support for maritime expeditions ended. Even though some high-seas expeditions took place afterward, the practice of private and government financing ended.[49] Thirteen years later, the Ming Dynasty prohibited the construction of oceangoing vessels. Local resources were to be used for pacifying the nomads of the steppes and for bringing about internal peace. In the classic Confucian tradition, social order was to be maintained through the good example of the authorities, and through legitimate rituals, without foreign influences. China had decided to isolate itself at a time when it was the most powerful and most advanced nation of the world. Not only did the high-seas expeditions cease, but maritime technology gradually deteriorated. These facts support the assertion that sporadic contacts with Asia could have existed until shortly before the European "discovery" of America.[50] In addition, there are well-documented experiences in Japan of several Japanese fishermen at the beginning of the seventeenth century whose rustic vessels were drawn by the winds and water currents to the American continent.[51] They arrived in the New World, independent of the fact that Columbus had discovered America. Likewise, Robert Heizer also has documented earlier visits by Japanese sailors to the western coast of North America, which they called Nootka, centuries before the first Europeans landed and even longer before anthropologists began their theorizing.[52]

With great perceptiveness, the American archeologist Betty J. Meggers has noted: "Many anthropologists are convinced not only that trans-Pacific contact took place, but that it occurred repeatedly and independently at different times on different parts of the western coast of the Americas. It should be emphasized that these contacts did not contribute significantly to the population of the New World, since such immigrants must have been few and their genetic composition would have been swamped by interbreeding with the local inhabitants. . . . It seems increasingly probable, however, that trans-Pacific introductions played an important part in shaping the civilizations that existed at the time of the European discovery."[53] Furthermore, Meggers and her collaborators claim that the Valdivia culture of Ecuador (3000 B.C.E.) has the same cultural origins as the Japanese Jomon culture.[54] Meggers also suggests that immigrants from the Chang civilization arrived in Mesoamerica at about 1200 B.C.E.[55]

From a strictly historical viewpoint, none of this evidence taken alone proves that Asians discovered America. But taken together, an accumulation of evidence clearly tells us about an Asian connection at important stages of Amerindian history. Modern science has at least two problems to confront: Either the first Asian immigrants to the New World were not as savage as has been presumed, or there were transpacific contacts with Asia when the ancient Amerindians had already ceased to be savages. One suspects that the evolution of Amerindian civilizations could include ingredients of both scenarios. Obviously, new frontiers of knowledge remain to be explored by industrious researchers in all the academic disciplines. In the meantime, it can be asserted that before 1492 the interrelationships between ancient Amerindians and peoples from other continents seem to have amounted to no more than a trickle compared to the mutual contacts of European, Asian, and African civilization centers. The oceans engulfed the Americas in an immense isolation while they were in the process of developing their own civilizations.

The question of who the "Indians" were, and where they originated, fascinated the first Spanish explorers and continues to fascinate modern researchers. Among the more exotic views about the Indians were those of the Spanish monk Juan de Torquemada, who in 1613 suggested that the Indians had originally been Carthaginians and Phoenicians, and supported his thesis by citing the similarities between the Phoenician and the Aztec religious rites of human sacrifice. The Mormon patriarch Joseph Smith (1805–1844) believed that the Indians were the descendants of one of the lost Ten Tribes of Israel. The Dutch historian Hugo Grotius (1583–1645) suggested that the North American Indians came from Norway, those of Yucatán from Ethiopia, and those of Peru from China. This exoticism can be explained partly by the fact that it was not until the eighteenth century that the Swedish scientist Carl Linneus invented a fourth human race: the red man.[56] Linneus was a better botanist than anthropologist.

More recently, science fiction writers Eric Von Daniken, Alan and Sally Landsburg, Rod Serling, and others have suggested that the more technologically advanced Indians came from outer space.[57] Although such fantastic theories cause disdain and even laughter in many academic circles, they have a serious obscurantist impact among average citizens. More significant, they not only sanction the intellectual limitations attributed to the ancient Amerindians, but also undermine their creative accomplishments. Since these science fiction books sell by the millions, it is important that the academic community take a stand against such commercialism, which has produced fortunes mostly at the expense of non-Whites.

Pre-Columbian ceramic of Asiatic
style found in Ecuador.

Pre-Columbian stone sculpture
of Asiatic style found in Mexico.

Nazca ceramic (Peru) with Chinese letters. See Dennis Lou, "Chinese Inscriptions
Found in Pre-Columbian Objects," *XXXVII Congreso internacional de
Americanistas: Actas y memorias*, vol. 4 (Buenos Aires, 1968), 179–184.

Pictography in Quebrada de Palo (Chancay, Peru).
With the aid of Professor Saturo Kumano, Nagoya University (Japan),
the written signs have been identified as being derived from ancient Asia.

Researchers at Beijing University (China) assert that Fusang also included the
Bay of Paracas (Peru). See Song Boozhong and Wang Dayaou, "Antiguas relaciones
entre China y Perú," *Debate* (Buenos Aires) 7 (24) (October–November 1994): 48.

Visitors who came by sea with the dragon symbol
(pre-Classic Mesoamerican period, 200 B.C.E. to 200 C.E.),
Izapa, Chiapas, Mexico. See Paul Chao, *The Origin of Ancient
American Cultures* (Ames, Iowa, 1983), 108.

Chinese ship from the early fifteenth century of 400 feet as compared
with the *Santa María* (85 feet) of Christopher Columbus.
See Louise Levathes, *When China Ruled the Seas* (New York, 1994), 21.

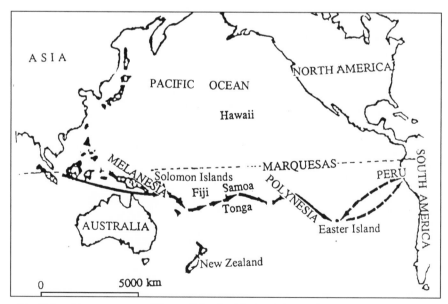

Pre-Columbian contacts of Easter Island with the Asian and American continents.

DIFFUSIONISM VERSUS ISOLATIONISM

Despite the variety of accounts of the Indians and their cultures since the discovery of America by the Europeans, there are two basic schools of thought that have debated the question of Indian backwardness or sophistication. The so-called Diffusionist School maintains that the Amerindians were not capable of erecting the more spectacular ruins scattered throughout the Americas and argues that those remains are the products of people and ideas that originated somewhere else. On the other hand, the Isolationist School considers the pre-Hispanic archeological remnants to be the products of purely local efforts, without significant foreign influence. This debate has been characterized by racist implications and defensive chauvinism, as well as by the fact that many debaters seem to be trying to prove whether the egg or the chicken came first. Implicitly and explicitly, such a polemic assumes that the Amerindians were unable to maintain a cultural and scientific dialogue. Indeed, it should be understood that the Amerindians were no less creative than any other so-called "race," and that they developed their own lifestyles in their own environment. Fortunately, this controversy has its greatest problems and debates among the doctrinaire dogmatists at each end of the issue. The heart of the problem is a simple one: Did the Indians have the technology, labor organization, and cultural sophistication to build the great cities, monuments, aqueducts, and other engineering marvels found in the New World?

In the twentieth century, modern archeology has come to the aid of the Diffusionists and Isolationists alike, endorsing many of their pronouncements. However, the application of modern archeology to

Latin American cultures is still in its infancy. It is probable that count-
less ancient ruins of great significance are still buried in unexplored
and uncharted areas. Thus, any theoretical assumptions run the omi-
nous risk of being dramatically debunked in the not-so-distant future.
Those who participate in the debate about diffusionism and isolationism should remember that in terms of a more global and long-term
vision, the more advanced pre-Columbian cultures were connected
geographically to Asia, and to Europe.

Why is it that so many exotic accounts of the Indians have persisted? This is partly due to the fact that from the conquest onward,
Indians have been mostly defined by what white people thought of
them rather than what they thought about themselves—including
the use of the term Indian itself. As the American anthropologist
Frederick Peterson has noted, "Most of us were once prone to believe
that all European and Asiatic cultures were far superior to the indigenous cultures of Pre-Columbian America. This ethnocentric view
stemmed from our European heritage and cultural affiliations."[58]
There has been much reluctance to perceive the Indian as anything
other than a primitive savage. Consequently, whenever Indians were
demonstrated to have accomplished something analogous to, if not
more advanced than, a Western civilization's equivalent accomplish-
ment, Westerners easily convinced themselves that the Indians must
have acquired it from somebody else. In other words, the lack of evidence itself was used as verification of the contrary.

RELIGIOUS FANATICISM

The conquistadores and the subsequent groups of white settlers who migrated to America were neither anthropologists nor ethnologists. They had very little patience for anything that was contradictory to their own economic security and spiritual values. Many priests and missionaries who went to America to "convert the heathens" perceived striking similarities between Indian cultures and that of the biblical Hebrews. Such discoveries did nothing to prevent the clerics from imposing policies of forced labor or to deter the new settlers from trying to wrest political and economic control of the area from the Indians. Even those who studied and recorded Indian traditions had not overcome prejudices and outright racism. For example, much of what we know about the Mayas' daily life at the time of the conquest is based on the observations of the priest Diego de Landa,[59] who openly despised the Indians, and even burned their sacred books. Self-styled "protectors of Indians" like Las Casas were a minuscule number who were more often ridiculed than listened to. Even the famous Spanish savant and historian Ramón Menéndez Pidal could not separate himself from his Hispanist chauvinism and in 1963 attacked Las Casas as a "pathological liar."[60]

An examination of the Amerindians from a more humanist perspective reveals that within the context of their own social structures, they were well-integrated, functional individuals. The Amerindians were a vigorous people with an admirable spiritual harmony. This is particularly remarkable in view of the physical and mental dislocation inflicted on them after the arrival of Western civilization in the New World. Europeans, in part due to greater contact with other civilizations outside their own continent, to the presence of draft animals, and to superior firearms, benefited from an advanced technological capability. But in the area of knowledge and ethical values, Amerindians were on a par with Europe, if not more highly developed. Obviously, technological superiority and cultural superiority are not necessarily connected, but that is something that we are just now discovering. It is significant that Amerindian technological knowledge was sufficient to give their societies a higher standard of living than the invaders allowed them after the conquest.

Indians were not Noble Savages either. Within the context of their immediate environment, Indians were no less irrational than their European counterparts. Amerindians included a wide range of personalities, from astronomers, philosophers, poets, and engineers to liturgical cannibals. Their descendants who survived came from primitive people as well as from kings, queens, nobles, merchants, artisans, peasants, and slaves. In America as in the Old World, state and stateless societies coexisted side by side—indeed, they represented the entire kaleidoscope of human behavior and creation. Both Indians and Europeans were ruled by mystical Citizen Gods who claimed direct descent or appointment from their deities and ruled in their names while presiding over socioeconomic structures that imposed inequitable laws and an unequal distribution of resources.

HUMAN SACRIFICE

It has often been asserted that Christianity fought for the good against the paganism of the Amerindians, but the conquerors were hardly notorious for their ethical religious practices. For example, in 1562, Franciscan friars used torture to force Mayan priests to admit that they practiced human sacrifice. Historian Inga Clendinnen considers the allegations of human sacrifice in the water wells (*cenotes*) to be a historiographical fiction constructed by the friars as an elaboration on the inventions of tortured Indians. With regard to the existence of other types of human sacrifice, Clendinnen asserts: "There are at least, the same arguments to conclude the contrary."[61] Indeed, it was Iberian Catholicism with its Inquisition, religious fanaticism, exorcisms, omens, superstitions, and the dogmatism of the Counter-Reformation that redirected the spiritual world of the Indians, while their bodies were led into European modes of production.

Both Christians and Indians, despite the presence of numerous saints and virgins in Europe and the almost animistic indigenous worship of nature, were essentially monotheistic. Both could distinguish very clearly what was good and bad. Whites as well as Indians had profound concepts of good and evil in their mythologies, symbols, and metaphors. From the plains of North America and the Amazon forests to the high civilizations of Mesoamerica and the Andes, Amerindians engaged in mystical monologues that questioned their spiritual existence and asked for guidance from Huaka Tanka (the Great Spirit).[62] According to the *Popol Vuh*, the sacred book of the Mayas, while many gods are worshiped, there is likewise the one "great creator and protector god."

Unfortunately, several Indian tribes and especially the Aztecs did not confine the ancient religious human sacrifice to a symbolic level.[63] As in the old Christian communion, Amerindian religious sacrifice was part of a cult and ideology that justified bloodshed. Since most victims were war prisoners sacrificed in the name of Huitzilopochtli (Master of the Sun and God of War), such a bloody practice was intimately related to the ancient causes of war, and consequently it must be explained and understood in that context. As R. C. Padden has carefully explained, that cult was intimately linked to the maintenance of Aztec imperialism.[64]

Some victims were selected by the clergy, some were slaves acquired for the occasion, and others were common criminals. The number of executions by this method is a matter of dispute among historians, and the number posited depends on European sympathy or antipathy for the Indians. The first bishop of Mexico, Juan de Zumárraga, stated that in the Aztec capital twenty thousand people were sacrificed annually, while Hernán Cortés's secretary, who never visited America, noted more than fifty thousand per year. On the other hand, Las Casas set the figure at around one hundred annually.[65] The controversy about this mysterious practice originated during Columbus's second trip to America, because it became necessary to find a moral reason to justify the imposition of Spanish colonialism. During the three months that Columbus spent in the Caribbean on his first trip, he saw neither human sacrifice nor cannibalism. In fact, Columbus explicitly denied the European expectation of such practices by the natives.[66]

The descriptions of human sacrifice have been mixed with those of the presumed cannibalism of the Amerindians. Western scholars have theorized with great subtlety[67] and naïveté about the symbolic and semisymbolic ceremonies that involved this horrifying practice. Aztec efforts to survive among hostile neighbors in a hazardous environment had much to do with their bloody mystical death cult. They were strict disciplinarians with drastic social laws. Their sacrifices were made by bloodletting, beheading, and sometimes by extraction of the heart. The fact that the Mexican highlands had seen one of the major demographic explosions in the world between 1350 and 1519

C.E.[68] did nothing to discourage the practice of human sacrifice.

The American anthropologist T. D. Steward suggests that the persistence of human sacrifice may have been the result of the social urge to provide a serious check on the population growth.[69] Human sacrifices have been present in the most ancient agricultural societies. Competition among early people for more fertile lands became a constant source of escalating warfare; hunger and fear of hunger was deeply ingrained in human psychology and in the search for the supernatural. The religion of primitive people was intimately related to their quest for food.[70] Apparently, human sacrifice was indeed practiced by the Aztecs, and it is also possible that such practices had taken place among other Mesoamerican ethnic groups, but not necessarily at the time of the Spanish conquest. By modern standards, human sacrifice and all its bizarre implications seem to be irrational and cruel, comparable to the brutal execution of almost half a million Europeans accused of being witches from the fifteenth to the seventeenth centuries.[71] Certainly, the recurrent theme of human sacrifice in Western historiography is not free of ideological and cultural axioms as well as biases.

THE MAYAS

Archeological research is a very expensive scientific activity, so our knowledge about ancient Amerindians has basically been determined by what has come to the attention of the international scientific community. As in other disciplines that study Latin America, American scholars have been the most active. European and, lately, Japanese scientists have also joined the field. The greatest level of interest has been the study of Aztecs, Mayas, and Incas, so we know more about them than about other groups. Furthermore, American interest as well as the support of the Mexican government, which since the 1910 revolution has been trying to revive its Indian past, have contributed to the fact that our knowledge about Mesoamerica surpasses significantly what we know about the other ancient Amerindians. So far, the relative abundance of archeological data has suffered from the lack of debate between American and Mexican scholars. Perceptively, the Mexican historian Enrique Florescano has noted that the abyss between archeologists from both sides of the border "has widened in a spectacular manner,"[72] with negative results for science and history.

The origin and collapse of the Mayan civilization still remains clouded by an aura of mystery, and there is an ongoing lively scholarly debate on these issues.[73] The confusion remains despite the fact that the Mayas had the most advanced writing system among the ancient Amerindians. The Mayan language is characterized by its pictographic, ideographic, and phonetic nature. Unfortunately, most Mayan writings and books were destroyed or burned as a result of the fanaticism of the conquering Christians. Despite the efforts by the

American epigrapher Linda Schele, the four remaining manuscripts have not been completely deciphered. A Rosetta Stone has not yet been found by Western scholars, and it appears unlikely that this will occur in the near future. Sophisticated computer programs have been of great help in deciphering the hieroglyphs, even though the spirit of a language can not be completely understood that way. Researchers who study Amerindian languages and writings have found striking similarities with Asian languages and writings. Both the Mayan language and the more advanced Mesoamerican languages are written like Chinese: from top to bottom.[74]

Mayan hieroglyphs have constituted one of the greatest enigmas for Americanist Western scholars, but thanks to the pioneering efforts of the Russian scientist Yuri V. Knórozov, it has been possible to advance in deciphering these ancient texts. Knórozov maintained from the beginning that Mayan writing, like Chinese, combined pictographic, ideographic, and phonetic elements at the same time.[75] The Mayan and Chinese languages also are basically monosyllabic and logographic. In addition, all Mayan dialects have linguistic structures significantly similar to that of Japanese.[76] According to French scholar Paul Arnold, Mayan signs are very similar to those used in China from two thousand to one thousand years B.C.E. Furthermore, Mayan manuscripts, like religious Chinese and Japanese texts, were written with long-hair brushes. The comparison to old Chinese texts enabled Arnold to translate part of the Mayan manuscripts found the libraries of Dresden, Madrid, and Paris.[77] The Mayan hieroglyphs that have been translated so far concern the dynastic, political, military, and religious matters of the ruling elites, while the history of peasants, artisans, and small merchants remains in deep obscurity.[78] Since Mayan and Mesoamerican glyphs have nothing in common with European writing, perhaps a more fruitful solution to this enigma could result by tackling the problem from the perspective of oriental scholarship.

The name Maya itself is an invention of the white man; to be sure, the Mayas knew each other by different names. Many Mayanists trace Mayan origins to the mysterious Olmecs (also the indirect ancestors of the Toltecs and Aztecs) who inhabited the Gulf Coast of Mexico in the neighborhood of Tabasco and Veracruz at about 1200 B.C.E.[79] The

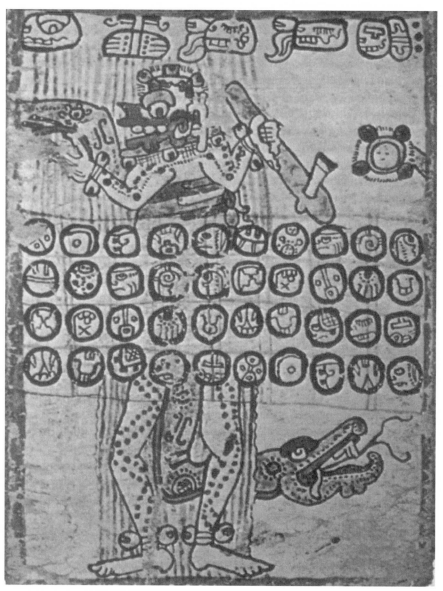

Mayan writing.

Olmecs linked almost all of Central America in a trade network. They were the first to use hieroglyphs, the vigesimal system, and the Mesoamerican calendar. The Olmecs produced the oldest and most sophisticated Mesoamerican art, which influenced the styles of the Mayas, Toltecs, and Aztecs. Olmec art includes sculptures of dragons, birds, midgets, hunchbacks, jaguars, anthropomorphic figures, and figures with anatomic organs. In addition to building great pyramids, the Olmecs sculpted gigantic stone heads, weighing as much as eighteen tons, on which can be seen Asian, Negroid, or Australoid faces. Olmec culture expanded to present-day Guatemala, Honduras, British Honduras, El Salvador, and Costa Rica, but the Olmecs mysteriously disappeared by the third century B.C.E.

The Mayas emerged as a distinctive culture in the fertile lowlands of Petén (Guatemala) in about the ninth century B.C.E.[80] It was the region with the most abundant and purest salt in ancient Mesoamerica. Mayan civilization reached its highest splendor between 250 and 950 C.E., an era often labeled as the Classic Period of Mayan and Mesoamerican history. During the height of this epoch, something resembling the ancient Greek city-states developed in an area of approximately 125,000 square miles comprising what is today south and southeastern Mexico, Guatemala, Honduras, and British Honduras. The most widely accepted population estimate is still that of Eric Thompson, who asserts that there were three million inhabitants in 800 C.E. By then, Tikal (in Petén), one of the biggest Mayan cities, had more than ten thousand inhabitants. The majority of the Mayas were peasants, but their cities were centers for worship, administration, and commerce. During the golden age of Mayan civilization, the major urban centers such as Tikal, Copán, Chichén Itzá, and Palenque were connected by masonry causeways and gravel or stone roads. Within the world of the Pax Mayana there were also conspiracies, conflicts, wars of conquest, and alliances among the city-states.

The Mayas derived their living from agriculture, but there was an entrepreneurial elite of shamans who profited from trade and agriculture. These merchants used red shells and corals from the Pacific coast as money.[81] This merchant elite survived even after the decline of Mayan civilization, until the Spanish conquest. Bishop Diego de

Mesoamerican places cited in the text.

Landa (1524–1579) describes them in the following terms: "In their markets, they traded in everything which existed in the country. They gave credit, lent and paid courteously and without usury. And the greatest number were the cultivators and men who apply themselves to harvesting the maize and other grains, which they keep in fine underground places and granaries, so as to be able to sell at the proper time. Their mules and donkeys are the people themselves."[82]

Among themselves the Mayas traded salt, calcium, cacao, obsidian, feathers, hides, textiles, ceramics, woods, medicinal herbs, natural crystals, and rubber. Despite the fact that they did not produce artificial glass, they shaped rock crystals into sculptures and utensils. Rubber was formed not only into balls and dolls but also into syringes used for enemas. The Mayas, along with other natives of tropical America, were the first people to use rubber for a multitude of purposes. The Mayas also engaged in trade outside their own territory, thus obtaining jade from Teotihuacán (about thirty miles northeast of Mexico City), and other tribes of modern Mexico.[83] They were seafarers and traded with the Caribbean islands, Panama, Colombia, Ecuador, and Peru. From South America, they obtained mostly gold, silver, and metallic alloys.[84]

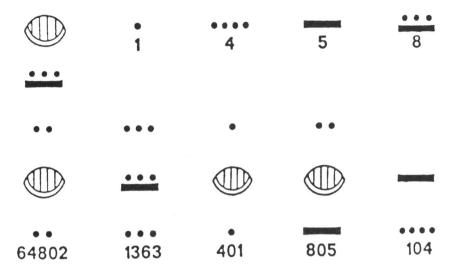

The Mayan numerical system uses as a base the number 20. The numbers are formed through the combination of points, lines, and the figure of a sea shell. A point is the equivalent of a unit. A line is the same as five units, and the shell represents the numeral 0. The basic column contains quantities that can reach up to 20. The following horizontal column contains numbers between 20 and 399. The subsequent column contains the numbers 400 through 7,999. Every new column increases 20 times every one of the numbers in the previous column.

Before the Christian era, the Mayas invented a yearly calendar that eventually became more accurate than the one used in Europe until the late sixteenth century; it was, in fact, accurate to within seventeen seconds over a period of 365 days. Our modern calendar consists of a year of 365.245 days with a margin of one day and a half every five thousand years, but the Mayan astronomical year of 365.2420 days was accurate within a day during the same millennium. At least from the beginning of the Christian era, the Mayas had a number system that included the concept of zero, an achievement shared by the Hindus, from whom the Europeans derived the idea. It is possible that Mayan mathematicians had conceived of zero at least five hundred years before the Hindus, but the idea of zero did not reach Europe until 1202 C.E. Modern researchers have pointed out that the logic of the Mayan mathematical system coincides with the algebra of George

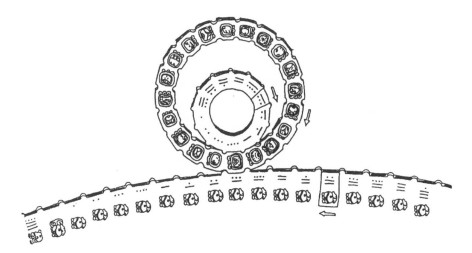

The Mayan conception of time.

Mayan astronomical observatory.

Boole, which is the technical base for modern computers.[85] The Mayan vigesimal system also has great similarity to the magical changes and calculations of the Chinese I-Ching.[86]

Mayan mathematical knowledge was developed because the high priests and intellectuals considered it necessary for divinations and astronomical observations. Mayan scientists conceptualized the earth as round.[87] The study of time became their biggest obsession. For the Mayas neither present, past, nor future existed as separate realities but were all part of an ongoing infinite cycle. The theocratic establishment charted every day of the year according to the position of the stars. Besides informing their disciples and believers about lucky and unlucky days, they also predicted eclipses, rains, and other natural phenomena. According to the mystical Mayan calculations, the world should reach the end of the world as it is now on Sunday, December 23, 2012.

On a more practical level, the Mayan understanding of nature and the terrain allowed them to remove the fragile limestone shelves that exposed subterranean water tables, thus allowing rains to percolate through the porous limestone. Mayan water reservoirs, cisterns, and irrigation systems remain as clear evidence of the way they coordinated their way of life with nature. Modern efforts to drill for water in Tikal were abandoned when the depth of 320 feet was reached.[88] Until recently, there has been much perplexity among Mayanists about the Mayan ability to cultivate high yields of food for a dense population, but thanks to space and aerial photography, it has been possible to conclude that the peasants dug an intricate network of parallel canals in the swamps. They placed the excavated soil onto the areas between the canals, thus creating a series of elevated gardens. Such practices supplied plants with only the amount of water that they needed, thus prevented the rotting of roots from an excess of moisture. The Mayas of the lowland tropical zones laboriously gathered and stored water in *cenotes* (wells), while those of the highlands built aqueducts. It was labor-intensive agriculture.[89]

It is difficult to know, in historical terms, how labor was regulated in Mayan society. Some early Spanish accounts, as well as archeological and anthropological data, indicate that Mayan society was hierarchical, providing abundantly for the theocratic elite and providing well for the majority of its agricultural population. This was a nonegalitarian society that included slavery. Slaves were either war captives or people who had committed infractions against certain social norms. Although they were bought and sold, they could own property and had free time that they could use for their own benefit. The slaves were of two types: household slaves and those used in mass production, such as in the cultivation of cacao.[90]

Average Mayas had a social, moral, spiritual, and ceremonial perception of work. There was a spirit of obedience, which allowed the elite to direct by corvée the construction of pyramids, temples, urban centers, and irrigation systems. The land was owned communally by clans, which produced for themselves and rendered tribute to the theocratic elite. As Sylvanus Morley perceptively notes: "The mass of people ... were humble corn farmers, whose sweat and toil supported not only themselves but also their supreme ruler, their local lords and the priesthood. In addition ... they were the actual builders of the great ceremonial centers, the lofty pyramid temples, terraces, and raised stone highways which connected the principal cities. . . . And those same common folk were even beasts of burden who carried the stones from the quarries to the building sites."[91] This type of hierarchical social structure provides the biggest clue to the demise of the Mayan Classic Period.

By about 900 C.E., the lowland Mayan cities had been abandoned. The tropical jungle gradually covered them, preserving them for posterity. There was what has been termed a postclassic renaissance in Chichén Itzá and Yucatán, but what the Europeans found there was no longer strictly Mayan. The new sociopolitical organizations that were established in the Postclassic Period were without omnipresent kings and the rituals of absolutist hierarchical domination.[92] It was a mixed culture, the result of war and frequent occupations by the Toltecs of Mexico. British anthropologist Eric Thompson maintained that the Mayan collapse resulted from uprisings by peasants who resented excessive tributary requests by the ruling elites. Such revolts became the most decisive factors in the collapse of the classic Mayas. It was a social explosion. Further studies have confirmed that there was a collapse and virtual extermination of the theocratic elite rather than of the majority of the population.

The downfall of Mayan civilization must be examined within the context of contemporaneous ecological changes throughout Mesoamerica. The droughts of those years rendered useless the canals and aqueducts that served for transportation and irrigation. In addition to drought and other ecological changes,[93] there were invasions by northern tribes and defensive wars against those nomads. Those disturbances caused the Mayan system of trade to deteriorate further, causing scarcity and forming the basis for internal problems, which left them even more vulnerable to external attack.[94] Attacks by northern tribes further distracted the working masses from the elaborate chores that life in the steamy jungles demanded for agricultural production, and little by little the wild forest took over the area.

By about 800 C.E., Mayan civilization was one of most highly developed in existence. Despite the Mayas' decadent social structure, they were the high Amerindian culture that most successfully resisted the avalanche of the Spanish conquest. The Mayas, like the other great non-European civilizations that prospered during the first millennium C.E., had superior technology and infrastructure to those developing in Western Europe during that period. The impact of ecological changes on economic development by the end of the first millennium C.E. in Central Asia and the Americas has not yet been analyzed scientifically from a global perspective.[95]

THE AZTECS

It is likely that the ancient Mexicans were hunters who came from the north during the Paleolithic period not long after the first Asian migrations to the Western Hemisphere. It was in the eastern part of modern Mexico (Tamaulipas and Tehuacán) that they became farmers sometime between 5200 and 3400 B.C.E. By approximately 1200 B.C.E., organized religion had been established, as is evident from the ceremonial mounds that appeared at La Venta on the Gulf Coast, the Oaxaca Valley, and Lake Texcoco. During this period at La Venta, the still mysterious Olmec tribe also emerged with a culture far superior to that of the other Mesoamerican tribes. At the outset of the first millennium B.C.E., when most of Western Europe was still illiterate, the Olmec elite had designed a hieroglyphic script. They had sophisticated artistic talents so advanced as to suggest a long developmental period in Mexico or elsewhere. It has been asserted that the region where Olmecs emerged was the ecological equivalent of the Fertile Crescent of Mesopotamia.[96] They built their capital in a swampy area. Like the Peruvian Chavín of the same period, they worshiped the jaguar (the rain god), built pyramids, and sculpted large stones, with stylistic similarities of artistic detail. Such facts suggest at least some kind of casual contact.

Apparently the Olmec became the mother culture for all the higher cultures of the Mesoamerican Classic Period. The Mayas seem to have been direct descendants of the Olmecs, more successful in improving upon their cultural and technological legacies than the other peoples in the area. In the Mexican highlands to the north, Olmec scientific achievements did not flourish with such vigor.

During the Classic Period, agricultural production increased, and society became well structured, with a religious and military elite ruling over the peasantry. There were also small numbers of slaves, merchants, artisans, and minor officials. During this period, urban centers developed throughout what is now the Mexican republic, among them Monte Albán, El Tajín, Xochicalco, and Teotihuacán (the place of the gods). Teotihuacán was the most important religious center in the Mexican highlands during most of the Classic Period (approximately 300–750 C.E.). At its height, Teotihuacán reached 250,000 inhabitants (500 C.E.). It was one of the greatest cities of the world. The Mesoamerican obsidian industry, which fabricated arms and tools, was centered in Teotihuacán. This theocracy imposed a sort of Pax Teotihuacana throughout most of Mesoamerica. By the eighth century, in a process reminiscent of the fall of Rome, Teotihuacán was invaded by nomads from the north who also eventually deserted the city. Some of the Teotihuacán residents fled to the shores of Lake Texcoco, where they continued their culture and traditions. The downfall of Teotihuacán was typical of what was to occur by the close of the Classic Period in the other Mexican urban and religious centers. It was a period of turmoil, invasions, migrations, bloodshed, and ecological changes that engulfed most of Mesoamerica. From the ashes of such turbulence rose many new states controlled by the Toltecs, the Mixtecs, and the Aztecs, all in the central highlands.

The neophyte states of the central highlands were under constant attack by seminomadic invaders from the north, who raided their settlements and wrested control of the agricultural lands. The Aztecs called these relentless tribes, a Nahua-speaking ethnic group, Chichimecs (People of the Dog). Eventually these warlike people with various dialects settled down and adopted the culture of the conquered peoples. The Toltecs themselves were a Chichimec group who had come to the central highlands at an earlier time. With the advent of the barbarians, constant warfare became a way of life, and human sacrifice became an institutionalized part of their religion.

During the tenth century, the Toltecs founded their capital at Tula, fifty miles north of Mexico City. From Tula, they tried to control and establish hegemony in central Mexico. During the Toltec hegemony, metal tools began to be used in Mexico. Amerindian metallurgy had originated in the Andean region in an earlier period, and gradually extended itself northward. Gold, silver, copper, and alloys were used mostly as luxury goods and decoration, but metals were also used to produce needles, pliers, awls, hatchets, and the cutting edges of agricultural tools.[97]

According to legend, in the last third of the tenth century, a Toltec Citizen God and prophet took the name of the ancient deity Quetzalcoatl (Feathered Serpent), and ruled in his name. Quetzalcoatl distinguished himself by his piety and the teaching of better agricultural techniques. Like Akhnaton of Egypt, he tried to bring about a religious reformation. He wanted to end human sacrifice, and advocated that only snakes, flowers, incense, and tortillas should be offerings to the gods. Mainly due to such heresies, he was forced by a rival faction to abandon Tula. A myth was spread by the remaining followers of Quetzalcoatl that their hero had escaped by sea, promising to return and rule over his people once again. This myth was to be used advantageously by the conquering Spaniards, who also found it convenient to add the physical characteristic of whiteness to their vision of Quetzalcoatl. According to Mayan historical chronicles, in 987 c.e. a Toltec warrior named Kukul-Chan (Feathered Serpent) captured Chichén Itzá (Yucatán). He ruled for an undetermined period, but long enough to change the city's architecture and sculpture style as well as to introduce the cult of the Feathered Serpent deity.[98]

By the twelfth century, the Toltecs were also defeated in the central highlands by new waves of Chichimec barbarians, who burned and destroyed their main population centers, including the capital, Tula. Thereafter, until the rise of Aztec rule in the early fifteenth century, no single tribe dominated the Mexican highlands. The Aztecs were the last major Chichimec tribe to enter the Valley of Mexico during the twelfth and thirteenth centuries. The Aztecs came from the north, wandering for many years before they finally founded the city of Tenochtitlán in 1325.[99] The city was located on an island in Lake Texcoco, where the waters protected them from foreign attack. Afterward the Aztecs adopted the life of sedentary farmers. They developed trade and acquired the religion and culture of their neighbors. The official Aztec historiography, however, noted that the "chosen" Aztec people originated from the mythic land of Aztlán in 50 C.E.[100] Despite their dissimilar customs, the imperial ideology of the Aztecs, like that of their Incan contemporaries, maintained the idea that the Aztecs had introduced order and civilization in time and space.[101]

By the time of the Spanish conquest, the Aztec capital was one of the greatest cities of the world,[102] with more than three hundred thousand inhabitants, and the empire extended for about two hundred thousand square kilometers, with a total population ranging between six and fifteen million. Moreover, the total population of the central region of Mexico was over twenty-five million.[103] When the Spanish visited Tenochtitlán, they were astonished. Those who could write described it as like something in a fairy tale, and they claimed that neither Spain nor Europe had any city that could compare with the Aztec capital. The Spaniards noted that this orderly metropolis had no thieves on its streets, and that it was the most beautiful and cleanest city on earth. Tenochtitlán had an area of almost ten square kilometers. Transit in the city took place via streets, boulevards, and canals, where there were many gondolas and other boats. There were temples and palaces built of stones that were white or of exotic colors. The urban complex included monuments, schools, *cuicacalli* (singing houses), public buildings, residential districts, ball parks, botanical and zoological gardens, saunas, and all kinds of markets.[104]

The Aztec markets were adjunct mechanisms to the tributary social system. The sale and purchase of consumer goods, raw materials, and tools of production were politically and militarily controlled by the state.[105] The majority of the population in Tenochtitlán and the Aztec Empire were farmers. Perhaps the most sensational aspect of Aztec agriculture was the existence of floating gardens called *chinampas*. Modern scientists have calculated that for slash-and-burn agriculture, twelve hundred hectares of land are required annually to feed a hundred families properly. In the intensive agriculture of the chinampas, only between thirty-seven and seventy hectares are necessary.[106] In contemporary Tepoztlán, agricultural production with Aztec methods has yielded twice as much as with modern plowing.

The use of stakes, aqueducts, canals, dikes, and ramparts allowed the Aztecs to irrigate forests, chinampas, terraces, and high peaks, as well as to avoid soil erosion. The Aztec aquaculture ranged from algae (espirolina) and water-fly eggs to fish and ducks. As the American historian Charles Gibson has noted: "They built dams, causeways, aqueducts, canals, irrigation works, terracing systems, and cities situated partly in the water and partly on land. Fish and water birds helped to provide them with one of the most balanced diets in all America, and chinampa agriculture rivaled Asiatic rice-paddy cultivation in its intensity."[107] But as history was to witness, the advent of the plow, horses, sheep, and intensive mining soon brought barrenness to what was once fertile.

The Mayas had mathematical superiority in Mesoamerica, but the Aztecs also had a sophisticated mathematical system. They developed the idea of zero and used pictographic symbols. In many cases, the pictographic mathematics were combined with lines and points. As in all Mesoamerica, the Aztec arithmetic system used the number 20 as a base. In addition to making astronomical, astrological, and magical calculations, Aztec mathematics had practical functions in engineering, architecture, topography, administration, census, tribute, production, and trade.[108] The Aztecs had pictographic and logographic writing.[109]

In Aztec times, the land was worked collectively by communal clans, each consisting of a specific *calpulli* (ethnic group). The local community paid tribute to the political and religious bureaucrats with products and *cuatequil* (obligatory work) during certain times of the year. The majority of the calpulli's members belonged to the *macegual* (commoner) class. But internally, the stratified calpulli was not egalitarian; at the bottom there was a *submacegual* or *mayeque* class, analogous to European slaves in the system that existed during the same time period.[110] Recent estimates assert that up to 30 percent of the total population belonged to the submacegual class. In ancient Mexico, the slaves were not only prisoners taken in war; there was also a slave trade. The slaves were from both inside and outside the Aztec Empire. Although they could gain their freedom by purchase and through the grace of their masters, the masters had the power to kill them if they deemed it to be necessary.

The so-called flower wars that the Aztecs inflicted on their ene-mies were not total wars; they were opportunities to capture slaves. On certain occasions, within the context of the flower wars, ball games were agreed upon in which players could win the war, lose their lives, or be enslaved. The imperial Aztec mystic ideology was inti-mately related to the cosmological balance of positive and negative forces. From childhood, the Aztecs were educated to admire flowers and take care of the elderly, "and on the other hand, practice war, human sacrifices . . . and the death cult."[111] The American ethnohisto-rian Burr C. Brundage may be correct when he maintains that the Aztecs were never interested in a Pax Aztecana, because what the Aztecs least wanted was to coexist in peace with their neighbors.[112]

In the Aztec society, as in other Mesoamerican societies, there was a small intermediary class that included artists, artisans, and mer-chants. The merchants constituted a group that was growing in opu-lence and privileges. Cortés wrote that on his expedition from Mexi-co to Honduras, he and his entourage were quartered in great hostel-ries that belonged to merchants. These merchants had all kinds of employees, maids, and even excellent mapmakers (maids and map-makers could be either employees or slaves).[113] Cortés described a Mesoamerican magnate in the following terms: "He is the wealthiest merchant, and owns sea boats . . . he is very rich and is involved in the production of much merchandise so that even in the town of Nito, he had a district for manufacturing, and there, his brother was in charge of the business . . . among [his products] were cacao, cotton clothing, color dyes . . . ink, pitch pine for lighting . . . slaves, colored shells . . . gold . . . mixed with copper and other things."[114]

Mexican merchants had less political autonomy than their Euro-pean counterparts. In the tightly structured Aztec society, the mer-chants had a social status under the lower nobility, but above the commoners or agricultural plebeians.[115] The economic evolution of this social group is reminiscent of that in Asian societies. Despite the fact that, officially, the merchants rendered ceremonial tribute to the emperor, there already existed powerful magnates among them. These entrepreneurs were prohibited from looking at the emperor straight in the eye; they had to dress in humble attire in order to get an audience with him. The social position of the Aztec merchants was similar to that of their Japanese counterparts before the industrialization of Japan.

The Spanish conquerors perceived the commercial activity of the Aztec capital to be greater than that of Rome, Constantinople, and Salamanca; every day more than seventy thousand people bought and sold in the market. They traded through barter or by using cacao beans and strings of gold pieces. In the province of Tasco (on the Pacific coast), copper and tin coins were used.[116] Aztec merchants were already organized in powerful fraternities, and even had the goddess Yiacatecutli as their religious patron.[117] Cortés describes Aztec commercial activity:

Every trade and every kind of merchandise from all parts are found . . . jewelry of gold and silver, of bones, shells, corals and feathers; they sell stones, both rough and finished, adobes, bricks . . . . There is a place for animals where all kinds of birds are sold . . . they sell rabbits, hares, deer . . . There is also a wonderful variety of herbs, roots, leaves, and seeds which are sold for medicinal purposes. . . . There are barber shops where they wash and cut hair. . . . There are places where food and drinks are served for a price. There are porters like in Castile who carry loads for a price. . . . There are all kinds of vegetables . . . fruits. . . . They sell bee honey and from maize . . . they make wine which they sell. They sell all types of cotton of all colors. . . . They sell deerskins, raw or tanned . . . and of different colors. They sell much pottery of different clays and glazes and painted. They sell maize in grains and in bread. . . . They also make lacquer ware; they set and carve emeralds, turquoises, other precious stones and pearls. . . . They sell with much order and things are sold by units and weight . . . . certain men go around the market place as inspectors. There is one house where a dozen old men hear complaints and where all might see them.[118]

However, the market was insufficient to supply all the needs of the

Tribute register paid to the Aztecs by ethnic groups in the
Mexican central highlands. *Códice Mendoza*, No. 3552
(Biblioteca del Museo Nacional de Antropología, México, D.F.).

Aztec sauna bath. However, the perspective that the first Spanish
ideologists intended to represent with this illustration was a
type of Mesoamerican cannibalism. See *Codex Magliabecchi:
Libro de la vida que los indios antiguamente hazían y
superticiones y malos ritos que tenían y guardaban,*
edited by Zelia Nuttall (Berkeley, 1903), folio 65 (77).

Aztec metropolis. The tributes extracted from other regions subsidized the ruling class and its dependents.[119]

The Aztec emperor was treated almost as a divine being, and his
position was basically hereditary. However, the Council of Nobles,
together with the religious elite, had some influence in the choosing
of the new emperor. There was always more than one candidate
among the heirs of the previous monarch. The Aztec Empire itself was
the result of an alliance among three kingdoms. The state apparatus
had an authoritarian bureaucracy with active political, military, and
shamanistic roles. Every major population center had a *tlatoque*
(imperial headmaster), and his official bureaucrats were maintained
by communal tributes. Generally the position of tlatoque was hereditary. Many were relatives by blood or marriage with the imperial family. The high nobility owned private land, and some of them belonged
to military orders such as the Eagles and the Jaguars. They received
tributes in products and services from the macegual communities.[120]

The Aztec monarch lived in luxurious palaces, reminiscent of those of oriental despots. The royal table service was of gold, silver, and fine ceramics. For every dinner the chefs prepared more than thirty different courses; the banquets were shared by more than a thousand employees, guards, guests, and dignitaries. The diners were entertained by singers, other musicians, dancers, artists, jesters, and acrobats. Tobacco, refreshments, and *pulque* (cactus wine) were consumed. The emperor bathed thoroughly every day. He never wore the same clothes twice. Besides his legitimate wife, he had numerous concubines of royal blood.[121] It can be said, without overstating, that at least the head of the Aztec state had nothing do with the primitivism attributed to the ancient Amerindians. He was a person of exquisite tastes and supercivilized refinements.

THE INCAS

Before the discovery of carbon 14, archeologists studying the history of ancient Peru created chronologies more out of strong conviction than as a result of scientific research. Unfortunately, Peru has not yet been able to attract the attention that Latinamericanists have given to ancient Mesoamerica. Much remedial endeavor has been carried out by the American archeologist John Rowe, whose use of modern archeological techniques combined with the accounts left by the cronistas have allowed him to claim an "absolute chronology" in the study of pre-Hispanic Incan history.[122] His conclusions, however, must be questioned on the grounds that much archeological work remains to be performed in the less geographically accessible but no less important areas. Despite the arrogance implicit in Rowe's claims, his research demonstrates that the Incas, like the Aztecs, made their biggest imperial expansion during the last century of their existence. This interdisciplinary perspective and Rowe's conclusions provoked a strong critique by the Swedish historian Åke Wedin, who accused him of an "amateur" use of historical sources. Although Wedin agreed with Rowe in the main, he suggested that the absolute chronology should be accepted only as archeological approximations instead of absolute factual historical data.[123] The Swedish historian Magnus Mörner generally agrees with the critique of Rowe by Wedin, but he asserts that the latter has omitted the use of the Incan *quilcas* (pictographic symbols) in his historical critique.[124] It is more constructive, however, to have an interdisciplinary perspective because it brings us closer to the historical backbone of what have been called "peoples without history." Among defeated peoples, history does not necessarily have

56

the same goals as those of a more refined society. Reality demands, at the very least, humility and mutual respect for the judgments of the various disciplines that try to untangle the puzzle of the "peoples without history."

Before the rise of the Inca Empire, also called the Tawantinsuyo, there were two basic periods of Andean history. The Chavín appeared at about 1200 B.C.E. in the central Andes (Ancash).[125] The Tiahuanaco emerged in the Bolivian highlands at almost the same time as the Mesoamerican Classic Period, and it had declined suddenly by the end of the first millennium C.E. These mother cultures were the nuclear centers of diffusion in the Andean region and in western South America. The Chavín are contemporaneous with the Olmecs of Mexico, and they have striking similarities. The Tiahuanaco worshiped the sun, had monumental architecture, used copper and bronze, and worked the land collectively. The Chavín and the Tiahuanaco expanded in the Andes and toward the Pacific, but both civilizations reached their highest level of development in the mountains. With the decline of the Tiahuanaco, several new kingdoms emerged such as the Huari (Ayacucho) in the Andes and the Chincha and Chimu on the Pacific coast. The rise and fall of these kingdoms occurred almost parallel with the history of the Toltecs in Mexico. However, it was only with the advent of the Incas that some sort of Pax Romana was imposed in western South America.

No other Amerindian civilization reached the socioeconomic and political cohesiveness that the Inca Empire had achieved at the time of the arrival of the Spanish. The Tawantinsuyo extended from the San Juan River in southwestern Colombia to the Maule River in central Chile, and it included most of modern Ecuador, Peru, Bolivia, and northwestern Argentina. According to some measures, the Inca Empire extended from the third parallel of north latitude to the thirty-sixth parallel in the south, and it stretched for more than four thousand kilometers in longitude to include about 1,800,000 square kilometers with approximately thirty million people.[126] However, the American anthropologist Henry Dobyns has calculated up to thirty-seven million inhabitants,[127] while his compatriot Noble Cook asserts only nine million.[128] Dobyns maintains that due to European plagues,

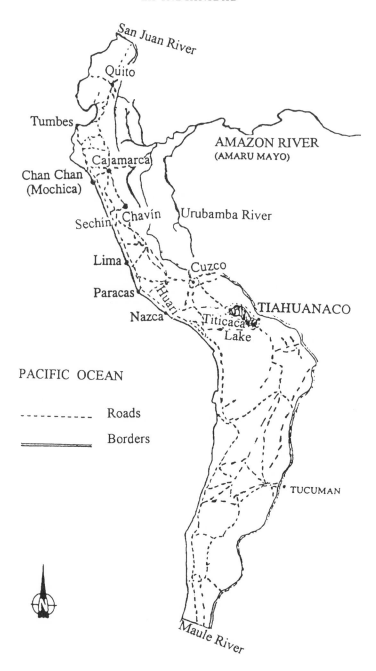

Main roads of the Inca Empire.

which reached the Tawantinsuyo before the arrival of Pizarro, the Incan population had already been reduced by fifty percent in the early 1530s.[129] Within the Inca Empire there were more than one hundred ethnic groups, and the dominating languages were Quechua and Aymara. The imperial apparatus ruled almost two hundred small kingdoms.[130] The Tawantinsuyo was the largest Amerindian empire, and its influence extended beyond its borders. Indeed, it was bigger than the Roman Empire at its maximum extension.

The Incan society was established between the twelfth and thirteenth centuries C.E. by the mythological Manco Capac and his wife, Mama Ocllo. The Inca and the Coya, as they were called, were members of a Quechua-speaking tribe from Lake Titicaca, who claimed to be the living children of the sun. They and their followers wandered until they discovered the fertile lands of the Sacred Valley (Urubamba), where they founded Cuzco (the belly of the world) at 3,467 meters of altitude. The capital of the warlike empire had over one hundred thousand inhabitants when the Spanish arrived.

Much paper and ink have been used to discuss whether Inca society was collectivist, like all early societies, or whether it was some kind of state socialism. Karl Marx thought that Amerindians lived as savages, but that the Andean and Mesoamerican peoples were only semisavages.[131] Within the context of classical Marxism, Rosa Luxemburg maintained that the Inca Empire represented the most advanced form of primitive communism, resulting from military conquests over other primitive communists. In addition, she asserted, Incan society represented the key to an understanding of primitive communism in the history of humanity and of all societies.[132] Despite this Western semantic classification, the Incas were neither savages nor primitives, so the unthinking application of such concepts must be avoided. What Marx least discussed was the so-called Asiatic Mode of Production. Whether because he died too early or because he was a European, he did not understand non-European matters very well.

The scholars who have analyzed the Andean socioeconomic relations most successfully, on the other hand, are precisely those who have analyzed the Asiatic mode of production. From a strictly historical perspective, no single theory can be used to explain the totality of history. Because history is too big, philosophical eclecticism is required. There is more than one reason to study the Amerindian cultures from the comparative perspective of the Asian world.

The Inca emperor had absolute hereditary power, but male primogeniture was not an automatic quality for succession. The heir had to be anointed by the ruling monarch as well. The cogovernment was created in order to avoid civil war and to facilitate the peaceful transition to the heir chosen by the emperor. After the time of Emperor Tupac Yupanqui (1447–1493), marriage between the emperor and one of his sisters was instituted in order to legitimize the succession.[133] The "sisters" of the Inca were in reality all the women of his generation within his ethnic clan. The emperor was considered a divine person and disobedience to him was sacrilegious. He was accepted as lord father and protector of his people, and after his death his mummy was placed in the Coricancha (Temple of the Sun), where he was worshiped together with the other deities of the Incan religion. Such a cult played a very important role in all levels of the Andean society. This cult was similar to ancestor worship in Asia.

The Incan emperor presided over the political-religious administration. He shared his tasks with the Uilla Umu (high priest), who was usually his brother or an immediate relative, and the Tucuiricuc (Imperial Council). The Coya was the personal advisor to the emperor, and she had important political-religious powers within the administrative hierarchy. There existed a bureaucracy whose highest levels were monopolized by the imperial family and the nobility of the conquered kingdoms. The administrative apparatus was organized in a decimal system. At the bottom of the organizational scale was the Chunka Camayoc, who was the chief of ten families and had authority over the communal lands they worked. The decimal system was implemented in order to synthesize the various sociopolitical structures of the conquered ethnic groups.

The advent of Incan hegemony brought the beginnings of land privatization at the top of the social scale. The Incas were benevolent rulers, but only the elite enjoyed a luxurious lifestyle with palaces, servants, polygamy, and the right to chew the best coca. At the other extreme of the social spectrum, the decimal collectivist system replaced the older communal organization based on family and ethnic links. Authority came from above and duty from below. The commoners were restricted to a monogamous existence and were subjected to different laws and moral codes from those governing the upper echelons of society. However, Incan society was flexible enough to permit males who distinguished themselves in the service of the emperor, especially soldiers, talented technicians, or artists, to rise up the social ladder. This was a situation in which the emperor could give everything and take all as well. Labor and upward loyalty were regulated under three major commandments: *Ama Sua* (do not steal), *Ama Quella* (do not be lazy), and *Ama Llulla* (do not lie). Infractions among the lower classes brought the death penalty for the culprit and his family. The growing social differentiation in the Inca Empire is perceptively stated by the Peruvian archeologist Luis G. Lumbreras: "The Incas were beginning to develop individual or family ownership forms of authentic feudal character."[134]

It is clear that the elaborately hierarchical Incan society, which supported an opulent ruling elite, knew no poverty. There was a myth of reciprocity between the rulers and the ruled.[135] Work was ceremoniously venerated at every social level. Everybody was required to produce according to his or her own abilities, but the elite had a greater choice as to how it would contribute to society. The state provided for the care of the sick, lame, elderly, orphans, and widows and widowers; even productive chores were designed for the lame and other disabled people who could still work. Indeed, the Inca Empire produced in abundance and accumulated reserves.[136] The Incan cultivation areas were greater than those of modern Peru, not only in the highlands but also in the arid coast as well. Likewise, the collapse of the Incan bureaucracy terminated the ecological administration of food production in the Tawantinsuyo. The comments of the American historian E. Bradford Burns are appropriate in this respect: "One must recall, as a point of comparison, that the vast and relatively populous Inca Empire fed its inhabitants well and maintained large food surpluses to compensate for lean years and natural disasters. That same area has been unable to do so since the Spanish conquest in the sixteenth century. In this particular case, we are challenged to under-

stand why Incan technology, efficiency, and productivity surpassed
Western technology, efficiency, and productivity or why the Inca
Empire of the fifteenth century was more developed than Peru, or
Ecuador or Bolivia of the twentieth century."[137]

The role of women in the Incan society was of great importance,
not only for their functions as mothers, wives, concubines, and working companions. Women made possible the reciprocity ritual between rulers and vassals. In the festivities, ceremonies, and rites of the
state, the emperor could invite his important guests to receive *chicha*
(corn beer), coca, and exotic gifts. In the Aclla Wasi (Home for Women), were produced fine textiles, chicha, and other drinks that
enabled the state to distribute reciprocities. The Aclla Wasi protected
different kinds of women. Generally the girls who joined the Aclla
Wasi were between eight and ten years old. They were from various
social classes and regions and had various personal qualifications and
physical appearances. Those of noble origin, the Yurac Aclla, were considered the wives of the sun and were to remain virgins; they were
dedicated to religious activities. The more beautiful women could
become secondary wives of the emperor or could be given in matri-
mony to his favorites and bureaucrats. As in ancient China, the courtly concubinage was rotated according to the lunar calendar.[138] The
women who were not distinguished for their origin or beauty remained as servants in the Aclla Wasi.[139]

Agriculture was the main occupation of Incan society. The Spanish
chroniclers were astonished by the abundance and surpluses of food
resources stored in depositories (*tambos* and *collcas*) during the conquest. By using foot-driven and hand-driven ploughs with metallic
ends (*chaki-taclla* and *maki-taclla*), guano fertilization, canals, aqueducts, and extensive terracing, the Incas managed to grow corn,
beans, tomatoes, fruit trees, cotton, tobacco, coca, and more than fifteen hundred varieties of potatoes. Like corn in Mesoamerica, the
potato in Peru was the basic staple diet. The agricultural production
in the highlands was not only for local consumption, but was used to
subsidize the coastal region, where due to the aridity of the desert,
some populations could produce only one third of their needs. The
rest was obtained from fishing and through barter.[140] The city of Jauja

Incan peasants.

in the central Andes, for example, was a *qhatu* (trade center) for Andean and coastal products; more than one hundred thousand persons bartered goods every day.[141] Since pre-Incan times, the coastal inhabitants had subsisted through trade, and used seashells as money. This proto-mercantile practice existed from Chincha to Mesoamerica.

The proximity of different altitudes and vertical ecological zones supported a sophisticated bureaucracy that collected and distributed goods in the Andean region.[142] Despite the fact that the bureaucratiz-

Houses of ancient Peru depicted on Mochica ceramics.

ing process was expanding, the productive unit was still the Ayllu
(family clan or ethnic group).[143] The value of production from the
Ayllu was divided in such a way as to leave enough for the needs of
the local community while the surplus went to the state and religious
authorities. Thus, the land was formally divided into three sections: for
the community, the state, and religion. The cultivation rested upon the
shoulders of the *runa* (average Incan citizen). The runa was also subjected to the *mita* and *minka*, which constituted obligatory work by
turn for the benefit of the community and the state during some periods of the year. During those periods, the runas might labor in the
mines and in the coca plantations as well as building roads, bridges,
temples, and other public facilities. The lands of the state were also
subdivided into three sections: common lands, those of the *panacas*
(royal clans), and the private lands of the emperor. Production from
the common lands covered the expenses of the administration of the
imperial apparatus. When the emperor died, his lands passed to his
royal clan. By the end of the Inca Empire there were twelve panacas.
With the development of the panacas, and the private property of the

ruling elite, emerged a class of *yanaconas* (semislaves or vassals). It is likely that the yanaconas composed the main working group in the private sector.[144]

In the Tawantinsuyo, the state demanded tribute in metals, precious stones, wild animals, and unusual objects. But that form of tribute could be done mostly by the *curacas* (nobility and local chiefs). No curaca could take office without being previously trained in Cuzco and accepted by the Incan elite. The Colombian historian Hermes Tovar Pinzón, as well as the American anthropologist John Murra, assert that the Incan state received most of its tribute in labor.[145] This emphasis on labor constitutes the great difference between the tributary systems of the Inca Empire and Mesoamerica. Chicha and music were fundamental to state labor in the Tawantinsuyo. The bureaucratic administration of production and labor in great scale permitted the Inca Empire to distribute food to all its inhabitants.

Although the subjugated tribes of the Aztec Empire were subjected to forced contributions of different kinds, they were allowed considerable freedom in their religious and socioeconomic organization.[146] The Aztec hierarchical system was less structured than that of Incan society. In the Aztec Empire, war and the threat of war kept vassals obedient. The death cult of the Mexican people was used by the state in order to control the conquest and growth of the Aztec Empire.[147] On the other hand, the Incan bureaucracy was more centralized, and it exercised great diplomatic skills in the conquest and global administration of conquered vassals. The Incas routinely used threats, demonstrations of power, and presents as an alternative to war, and they were distributors of goods. Those policies constituted the fundamental essence of the Incas' self-appointed civilizing mission. The Incas considered all the peoples outside their domain as barbarians. As soon as a new tribe or kingdom was incorporated, the cult to the sun god was forced on the neophyte vassals, but they were allowed to keep their local deities on a secondary level. The heirs of the local chiefdoms were taken as hostages to Cuzco, where they were inculcated with Incan traditions. In addition, a resettlement program was initiated whereby sizable numbers of the newly conquered

yanaconas were interspersed with *mitimaes* (loyal citizens). The mitimaes were not only good spies, but would teach the new vassals
Quechua and the Incan ways of doing things.

Despite the Incan assimilation policies, each individual had to
dress in the manner of his region and ethnic group. The local nobili-
ties were allowed to keep their privileges, and intermarriage with the
Incan nobility was permitted. Roads were built to connect the new
frontiers to the royal highways leading to Cuzco. But above all, a
social restructuring was effected in which the Incan tributary system
was implanted. As the German historian Friedrich Katz has noted, the
Incas were "takers" as well as "givers."[148] Indeed, Incan rule was an
enlightened despotism that had as its objectives the promotion of
some sort of social justice, a melting pot, pan-quechuaism, and the
Pax Incaica. On the other hand, the Aztecs subjugated many ethnic
groups without assimilating them; each ethnic group had its own
internal structure and government. The Aztecs imposed their norms
more by force than by persuasion.

The Incan Sciences

The technological knowledge acquired by the Incas was
unequaled by the other ancient Amerindians. Much of Incan technological superiority was due to their quickness in adopting the know-
how of their conquered vassals. Their roads, many of them forty feet
wide, reached all the corners of the empire, and were equipped with
stone bridges, pontoon bridges, suspended bridges, and hanging bas-
kets for carrying passengers over *oroyas* (rope bridges). Some of the
suspended bridges were over two hundred meters long,[149] and one of
them was in use until the end of the nineteenth century.[150] The oroyas
served as a kind of aerial cable, and some had the capacity to hold
four persons.[151] The roads were also equipped with inns and food
depositories at regular intervals. The length of the Incan roads surpassed those built by the Romans (almost 23,200 kilometers). Spanish
chroniclers were full of admiration for the spectacular Incan road
engineering, and wrote that it was superior to Roman or Egyptian

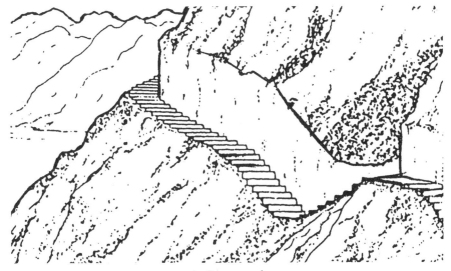

An Incan road.

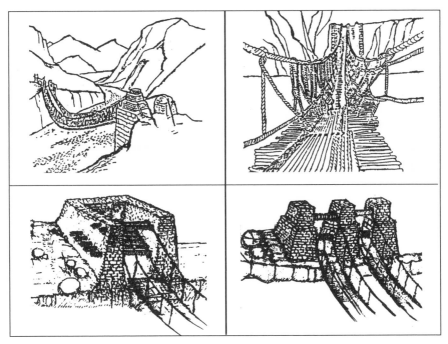

Incan hanging bridges.

The chasqui.

constructions, and that Charles V, despite his power, could never have ordered the construction of a road as good as the Andean roads. The case was made by the Spanish cronista Agustín de Zárate, who remarks that "none of the marvels of the world, which the ancient authors wrote about were built with so much difficulty."[152] The grandeur and length of the Incan roads continue to fascinate modern researchers. The American archeologist John Hyslop asserts that the Incan road system symbolized the omnipresence of state power.[153]

Over the Incan roads, products from the various regions of the empire were exchanged, armies moved, and the emperor and the royal official traveled. The roads facilitated the recruiting of the labor force. The roads also enabled the control of population movements, and the mail transport with its system of *chasquis* (relay carriers).[154] The chasquis were a vital factor in the global administration of the extensive empire. Some chasquis traveled by maritime routes as well.

Among the ancient Amerindians, the Incas had mastered the navigation of rivers, lakes, and the sea. Almost immediately after the Spanish captured the Panama isthmus, traffic of Incan vessels in the

Pacific Ocean was reported. The Incas built rafts of wood and *totora* (reeds) with sails. The biggest Incan vessels could transport more than thirty tons of freight and sixty passengers. These flat-bottomed ships were equipped with the *guara*, which enabled them to sail without leeway and change course through the winds and sea currents.[155] A replica of the guara was used by Thor Heyerdahl in his famous Kon-Tiki expedition from Peru to Polynesia in 1948.[156]

Incan stone masonry without the use of mortar was well adapted to the seismic nature of the Andes. The stones were so tightly set together that not even a razor blade could be placed between them. Many walls have since survived the fury of nature and the rampage of the conquest, while many Spanish buildings and walls have collapsed. Many Incan walls, which the Spanish could not dismantle to build their cathedrals and palaces, remain as silent testimony to Incan engineering.

Andean metallurgical techniques were developed independently from those of the Old World. Andean metallurgy was the most advanced of the Americas, and the Andes was the place where metallurgical technology originated in the New World, and from which it spread. During the first millennium C.E., the Andean peoples produced gold and platinum alloys, which was not accomplished in Europe until the eighteenth century. The Incas were aware of the expansion of metals caused by heat. They knew the effects of mercury, but its use was restricted because of its negative consequences for human health.[157] Researchers at the Massachusetts Institute of Technology concluded that Incan scientists used electrochemical techniques for metal-

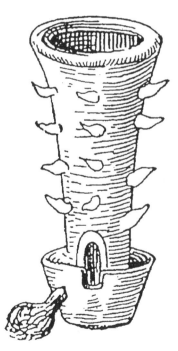

Incan furnace (guaira) for smelting metals.

lurgical lamination. Moreover, such Andean technology dates back to more than a millennium B.C.E.[158]

In order to smelt metals, the Incas preferred the use of *guairas* (small ovens), which were fueled by dry llama excrement mixed with *ichu* (puna straw). Those ovens were placed at the wind crossings and in the glens between mountains, and they were especially important when the winds were blowing with high intensity. The high temperatures produced by the guairas even made possible the smelting of meteoritic iron[159] and platinum.[160] Although from the perspective of the Spanish the guairas produced small quantities, their efficiency was so great that the conquerors continued to use them until the discovery of the patio process,[161] which used mercury to separate metals. The guairas smelted gold, silver, and copper, and produced a variety of alloys like *llasca*[162] and bronze. Llasca was composed mainly of zinc, copper, and lead. This alloy was used mostly for making agricultural tools. Moreover, in the coastal region, alloys of iron ore and bronze were produced from the beginnings of the common era.[163]

The Incas and the Andean peoples were also aware of the effects of refrigeration and natural dehydration. Such knowledge enabled them to store food as well as embalm their dead. The Incan embalming techniques are comparable only to those of the ancient Egyptians. Their knowledge of medicinal plants included the use of disinfectants, painkillers, and abortive herbs. Incan medicine men used coca, quinine, curare, and other products from the Amazon jungle. Andean pharmacology produced several types of penicillin from fermented potato fungi. This penicillin was ingested orally, nasally, and by enema in order to prevent or combat infections. Even today, this ancient medicinal practice is used by many Andean medicine men. Like Asian physicians, they practiced some type of acupuncture. Incan dentists used metal to crown teeth. Native medicine has had its most recognized merits in the field of neurology.[164] Several anthropologists and neurosurgeons claim that Incan doctors knew the craft of neurosurgery.[165] In addition to excellent surgical techniques, cranial trepanation required a deep knowledge of internal anatomy as well as of painkillers, disinfectants, and biological science. Judging from the numerous skulls that had undergone surgery, now displayed in Peru-

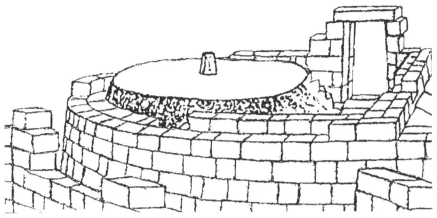

Intiwatana or Inca solar clock (Písac, Peru).

vian and foreign museums, the level of success was outstanding. These trepanation techniques expanded to Mesoamerica between the twelfth and the fourteenth centuries.[166]

Ancient Andean knowledge of medicinal herbs has survived up to the twenty-first century, and it is a medical and social alternative for the Peruvian lower classes, who cannot afford Western medicine. It is estimated that at least two-thirds of the Peruvian population benefit from this folk medicine. Only recently has native medicine begun to receive the attention of local academic institutions and medical schools. Scientific conferences and medical courses have included the participation of both medicine men and Western-trained doctors.[167] However, as the Canadian anthropologist Jeremy Narby has perceptively noted, the ancient Peruvian "illuminative wisdom" whose empirical results are used by the pharmaceutical industry "can not even be discussed scientifically because it contradicts the axioms of Western knowledge."[168]

The Incas' calendar was a system of constant readjustment based on twelve months of twenty-eight lunar days each. It was an agricultural calendar that, like those in Mesoamerica, had leftover days. The abundance of food in the Inca Empire made it possible to regard the extra days as times of good luck and festivities. The Incan concern for agriculture made these people study the stars, especially the movements of the sun and the solstice. From Cuzco to the Ecuadorial line (Rumicucho) there were *intiwatanas* (solar clocks) in every town that measured the different shades of sun during different hours, seasons of the year, and latitude grades.[169] Such observations suggest that the Incan astronomers and mathematicians like the Greek astronomer Erastosthenes (276–196 B.C.E.), conceived the earth as round.

The Andean textile industry was the most advanced of pre-Columbian America, and until the fourteenth century C.E., the textiles of Paracas and those of China were the most sophisticated in the world. The Andean textile industry was intimately intertwined with the development of symbolic and graphic communication. The *quipus* were woolen ropes of different colors from one to twenty feet long, from which hung thinner cords containing various knot forms. The more complex quipus included stone or wooden planks with some symbols to aid their decipherment. The quipus are considered to have been mnemonic devices that permitted the storage of various information sources, including historical, statistical, and mathematical data. Variants of the quipus were also common among the natives of Indochina, Melanesia, and Siberia. Thanks to the pioneering studies on the numerical quipus by the Swedish anthropologist Erland Nordenskiöld, the Western world was informed about the Incan conception of zero.[170]

The socialistic Incan state was deeply dependent on the statistical data stored in the quipus. The state had records of people, farmland, and important commodity stocks. Since the state collected taxes, regulated labor, and controlled trade, the use of statistics was most essential in allocating the resources of a collectivist society. Not only did each territorial unit of the empire keep its official quipus, but Cuzco had a sort of general data bank with vital records on production, population, and resource allocation.[171] Unfortunately, almost all the quipus were destroyed during the Spanish conquest. Their systematic burning was demanded by the Catholic clergy, who believed them to contain diabolic formulas.

The Writings of the Incas

The fact that an advanced civilization like Incan society did not seem to have had a system of writing has been a constant enigma for the international academic community. In reality, such a belief has simplified tasks for many researchers, since it could be argued that there was no more information because there were no written sources, and thus the only alternative was to begin with the arrival of European writing in Peru. Despite all that has been written by the victorious Spanish historians, evidence continues to support the hypothesis that in Incan times a writing system did indeed exist. Moreover, it is argued, a writing system may have existed in pre-Incan times. The word *quilca*, which literally means "writing," is found in pre-Hispanic Quechua and even in Aymara (*quellca*). These words existed in all their grammatical functions.[172]

When Hernán Cortés and his expedition arrived at the eastern Mexican coast, claiming to come with a message and greetings from the Spanish king, Charles V, the Aztec Emperor Montezuma sent Cortés an *amate* (pictographic canvas) welcoming and greeting him.[173] Likewise, when his cousin Francisco Pizarro appeared on the Peruvian coast with the same story, the Incan emperor Atahualpa sent him a quilca (like the amate, a pictographic canvas) welcoming him.[174] Unfortunately, Pizarro was illiterate, and his companions had a much lower literary capability than did the conquerors of the Aztec Empire. The conquest of Peru was not recorded by a masterful chronicler like Bernal Díaz del Castillo. Pizarro and his associates were very suspicious of those who could write, and of anything related to writing. Agustín de Zárate, to whom we owe much of what we know about the kidnapping of Atahualpa, went to Peru in the first years of the conquest as treasurer for Charles V. Even then the Pizarro brothers intimidated him, and he was prohibited from writing anything about the conquest during his stay in Peru.[175] Upon his return to Spain, Zárate published his chronicle, but only after it was censored by the Crown and the Inquisition. On another occasion, when Viceroy Francisco de Toledo exterminated the last Incan pockets of resistance in 1572, he also captured numerous quilcas.[176] The picto-

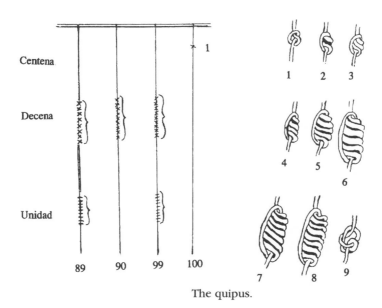

Centena

Decena

Unidad

89   90   99   100

1   2   3

4   5

6

7   8   9

The quipus.

The Quipu Camayoc.

The Quilca Camayoc at the
beginning of the colonial period.

graphic canvas sent by Atahualpa as well as the ones captured by Toledo were shipped to Spain, but they have never been found.[177]

The Spanish chroniclers have written that planks, canvas, and paintings ornamented with gold, explaining Incan history, were found in the Coricancha temple of Cuzco.[178] Of course, Spanish desire for the gold ornaments condemned those quilcas to disappear. Moreover, the Catholic priests and the inquisitors launched their infamous "extirpations" of idolatries by burning both quipus and quilcas. In Incan bureaucracy there were different officials (Quipu Camayoc and Quilca Camayoc) in charge of quipus and quilcas. Apparently the quipus were more widely used by the Andean masses, and that captivated the attention of the Spanish, but it is well accepted by researchers that Incan pictography was very advanced. In reality, it is not a question of whether the Incas had a graphic system of communication, but rather what was its level of sophistication.

The Incan chronicler Garcilaso de la Vega, who denies the existence of Incan writing, informs us that in the Incan solar clocks there were some "rude letters."[179] But in reality this Mestizo, who aspired to be Spaniard, conceived writing only in terms of Latin letters. Pedro Cieza de León, perhaps the most reliable of the Spanish chroniclers, noted that he had found hieroglyphic inscriptions on tiles near Cuzco, and that the natives translated them for him.[180] In 1652, the Spanish chronicler Fernando de Montesinos wrote, after living many years in Peru, that the Incas had a secret writing system that was limited only to the elite because they feared social upheavals.[181] Modern historians have ridiculed Montesinos for maintaining that the Incas were descended from one of the lost tribes of Israel. However, almost all the cronistas who pretended to write the history of the Amerindians from the beginning wrote within the biblical and religious context of human creation. Fortunately, archeologists and other scientists have found more truthfulness in the so-called fantasies of Montesinos. The Prussian scholar Alexander von Humboldt (1767–1835) claimed to have found hieroglyphic inscriptions in Peru.[182] Although not all the hieroglyphs and quilcas have been destroyed, even today most historians deny the existence of Incan writing.

In Peru, the study of pre-Columbian writing was begun by the archeologist Rafael Larco Hoyle. Through his research on symbols engraved in lima beans and on pictographs in ceramics, Larco Hoyle maintained that, indeed, there was a writing system in ancient Peru.[183] The efforts by Larco Hoyle were continued by the epigrapher Victoria de la Jara, in her study of quilcas in textiles and *keros* (ceremonial glasses) from the Andean region. De la Jara maintains that Incan writing is of a logographic nature, like that of the Chinese.[184] San Marcos University in Lima and other cultural institutions are also collecting quilcas and petroglyphs that remain in Peruvian territory.[185] Moreover, some Andean communities still collect, register, and transmit data in textiles. The historian Carlos Radicati, of San Marcos University, asserts that the quilcas and the quipus are intimately intertwined and that "they were modalities of the same writing."[186]

Until the Thirty-Ninth International Congress of Americanists (Lima, 1970), the international academic community in general had almost accepted as proven that the Incas had no writing system. During that meeting of great local publicity, a contingent of Peruvian researchers claimed that the Incan writing system had a symbolic and graphic character. Fortunately, on that occasion Peruvian academics had the official endorsement of German cryptologist Thomas Barthel of Tübingen University. Research about the Incan writing system continues in Peru and abroad. Both a phonetic and a numerical alphabet have already been produced.[187] These demonstrate the uniqueness of Incan writing.[188] The American anthropologist Gail Silverman asserts that the quipus and quilcas have a binary and ternary logic like that used in modern computers.[189]

The last word about Incan writing has not yet been said. Like many other Amerindian accomplishments that have been acknowledged during the last few years, Incan writing has yet to be examined completely. The history of the Amerindians does not end with the arrival of Western civilization in the New World. European written documents will add detail to the story of the process that almost exterminated the ancient Amerindians. However, Western historiography has been negligent in presenting the Amerindians within the total social spectrum that existed in the Americas. What Western historiography has tried to tell is the history of progress, but the history of Amerindians under the influence of Western civilization was not progressive; on the contrary, the encounter between Whites and Amerindians was like a hurricane that almost swept away Amerindian values and replaced them with the characteristics of Western civilization. What remains is mostly in the form of a subjugated culture that has endured centuries of attack. As a result of oppression and repression, only the essence of ancient dreams has survived. Even those last groups of so-called primitives who inhabit the Amazon rain forests seem doomed, as the idea of modernization continues to pervade the Americas under the influence of Western civilization.

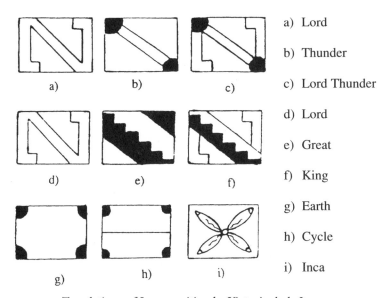

a) Lord

b) Thunder

c) Lord Thunder

d) Lord

e) Great

f) King

g) Earth

h) Cycle

i) Inca

Translations of Incan writing by Victoria de la Jara.

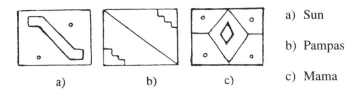

a) Sun

b) Pampas

c) Mama

Translations of Incan writing by Thomas Barthel.

Hieroglyphs of northern Peru.
See *El Comercio* (Lima), August 20, 1978, Sunday supplement, 10.

	Numeral	Number	Letters
	1	JUK	J
	2	KIMSA	LL-W-Y
	3	ISKAY	M
	4	TAWA	T
	5	PICHQA	R
	6	SOQTA	S
	7	QANCHIS	K-Q
	8	PUSAQ	P
	9	ISQON	N-ñ
	10	CHUNKA	CH

Incan numerical alphabet. See William Burns Glynn, "La escritura de los Incas,"
Boletín de Lima 12-14 (May–September, 1981): 19.

From Colonization
to Decolonization

One of the most difficult tasks for historians writing about the pre-Columbian past of the Americas is to determine how to be precise in diachronic terms. Not only did invaders and natives have different conceptions of time, but there are also limitations imposed by bad translations, varying cultural perspectives, and official history. For example, the primary sources from which a portrait of the Amerindians has been fashioned by ethnohistorians such as Miguel León-Portilla,[1] Nathan Wachtel, Edmundo Guillén, and others[2] are characterized by their long-term and institutional character rather than by diachronic exactness. My own efforts are exploratory at this stage; I am looking at this history from an Indian perspective so that the early process of European colonization can be analyzed chronologically. The observations presented here are based on documents and materials that are easily available to serious investigators.

THE CONQUEST REVISITED

It has been recorded that Christopher Columbus arrived at Samaná Island or San Salvador after thirty days on the high seas. What he found in the tropical Caribbean was a vigorous-looking race of naked or seminaked people. All the natives spoke the South American language called Arawak. They lived in towns of one to two thousand inhabitants, which were ruled by hereditary chiefs or *caciques* with varying levels of power.[3] Some of them exercised political influence in several islands. The Caribbean societies not only included Nitaínos, who were affluent and less affluent free individuals, but also a type of slaves known as Naborias. These societies had priests and shamans who took charge of their Zemis (deities) and their sacred places, and were also healers. The Caribbean natives lived from fishing, hunting, trading, and farming. In this last activity, women had a very active role, if not the dominant role. The natives had a sophisticated agriculture. For example, they built a series of *conucos*, elevated gardens of about a meter in height and three meters in diameter, in order to cultivate tubers. Such practice prevented soil erosion and facilitated irrigation in the tropical climate. In what is now Haiti, the natives had constructed extensive irrigation systems.[4] The local artisans were not full-time specialists:[5] they hammered gold and other metals, processed rubber for many purposes, produced ceramics, wove textiles, and carved wood, stones, bones, corals, and marine shells.

When Columbus first landed on American soil, the natives ran away because they feared slave-hunters from the Caribbean or the mainland. Only old men, old women, and children came out to welcome the foreigners.[6] After the strange visitors made it known that they were on a peaceful mission, a friendly dialogue took place. Within twenty-four hours of Columbus's arrival, the natives informed him that there existed a mainland to the west, and that a great ruler governed those parts. Naturally Columbus assumed that it was the Asian continent and that the ruler was the Great Khan.[7] It was, instead, a new continent, and the great ruler was the Aztec emperor. Before long, Columbus and his men were trading their trinkets for native nose- and earrings, armbands, and various ornaments made of *guanín*[8] and other metals, as well as precious stones and pearls. For the Indians, the precious metals and precious stones had only an artistic and cosmological value, not an economic one. The Europeans also obtained cotton blankets, textiles, hammocks, rubber products, feathers, and birds.

The Indians informed Columbus that the gold and precious stones came from the Caribbean southwest, and from what is now the island of Haiti.[9] Martín Alonzo de Pinzón, a lieutenant of Columbus, set out on his own with some Indian guides in the caravel *Pinta* to explore the Yucatan peninsula.[10] While Pinzón was away, Columbus explored Haiti and renamed the island Hispaniola. The island had fertile soil and the richest gold-bearing lands of the Caribbean.[11] Haiti was controlled by the family of the great cacique Caonabó, king of Maguana, and included the central and southern mountains of the island. In addition, Caonabó's wife, Anakaona, was the queen of eastern Cuba. The brother of the charismatic Anakaona was Behecchio, great cacique of Xaraguá in the southwest of Haiti. Columbus chose to befriend the cacique Guacanagarí, leader of the Taino people, who were enemies and tributary vassals of Caonabó and the Canibas or Caribas (Cannibals). For three months, Columbus managed to maintain cordial relations with Guacanagarí, but the gold-bearing lands were in the hands of Caonabó. Guacanagarí later fought on the side of the Spaniards to defeat the followers of Caonabó.

Archeologists assert that South Americans originally colonized the Caribbean thousands of years before the common era. Probably there was also a Mesoamerican migration, which would have arrived by way of the Yucatan peninsula. By the time Columbus arrived in the Caribbean, the Guanahatabeys of western Cuba would have been the only Central American ethnic group in the Caribbean. The rest of the native groups were Arawak speakers, of whom the Taínos were the majority. However, the Canibas and their allies were the dominant group militarily and the latest pre-Columbian immigrants. They concentrated themselves in the southern Caribbean and had Guadalupe and Martinique islands as their main centers. The Canibas were great merchants and controlled the contacts between the Caribbean islands and the northern South America mainland.

Archeologists and ethnohistorians specializing in the Caribbean have fewer primary sources to work with than their colleagues who study the rest of the American continent. We know most about the Tainos because the Europeans had more contacts with them, and because they were the allies of Columbus. The American archeologist Irving Rouse has classified the more advanced Tainos as the Classic Tainos. The Tainos of Hispaniola and Puerto Rico belonged to that category. However, as archeological explorations advance, other peoples like those of Jamaica have been elevated to the status of Classic Tainos.[12] This classificatory process by Western scholars clearly demonstrates how a lack of evidence continues to be perceived as proof of the contrary when the history of defeated peoples is studied.

The Canibas are perhaps the least known and most slandered Amerindians. The few European documents related to direct encounters with Canibas do not describe them as savage beasts. Instead they are portrayed as humans and even humanists.[13] Ethnically the Canibas were more mixed than the Tainos. Historical documents indicate that they had developed some technology that was superior to that of the Tainos. They were not savages. It is difficult to decide with scientific certainty who were the real Canibas and who were merely identified as such by the Whites in order to justify their own violence against the Indians; this is a great interdisciplinary and historiographic problem. The Canibas were the most difficult for the White man to defeat in the Caribbean. They gave asylum, first to Indians and afterward to African slaves who escaped from European brutality. They were the heroes of the Caribbean resistance. The Canibas of the Windward Islands resisted until 1797, when the British finally defeated them, and their survivors were removed to Central America.

Caniba spinners and weavers produced cotton blankets "that are so well woven that [they] in no way were inferior to those of our country," wrote Columbus.[14] They cultivated numerous fruit trees, and they traded their produce. In war, the Canibas used metal weapons and copper chest-protectors. Because of their use of curare as poison in their arrows and darts, they were victorious in many military conflicts.[15] The Canibas used iron tools on the island of Guadalupe, the only place in the Americas where this occurred, but the iron may have been of meteoritic origin; the letters of Columbus do not specify the type of iron used.[16] If it was meteoritic iron, it was likely imported from the Andean region.

Relations between Whites and Indians were most cordial during the first voyage of Columbus to the Americas. It was a relationship of mutual respect in which both parties enthusiastically traded with, played with, and learned from each other. When the time came for the Europeans to leave, forty volunteers decided to remain as the official guests of Chief Guacanagarí, while his brother and nephew, together with their maidservants and retainers, went to Spain as guests of Columbus.[17] Only six of the natives survived the trip to Europe. They were baptized in the Catholic Church, and the monarchs Ferdinand and Isabella became their godparents. One of them remained in Spain as a courtier until his death in 1495. The others returned with Columbus in order to help him conquer and pacify their Caribbean compatriots.

Before returning to Europe from his first trip to the New World, Columbus left all the trinkets brought in the caravels for the White volunteers to trade with the natives. He returned to Hispaniola after eleven months with more than twelve hundred Whites in seventeen ships loaded with trinkets, sugarcane, friars, horses, dogs, chickens, and all the necessary equipment to settle the land. Only three weeks before the return of Columbus, Caonabó and his army attacked the original Spanish settlement and their Taino allies. Contemporary documents that describe this first battle between Indians and Whites reveal that not all the Whites were killed. Moreover, some Spaniards had already left before Caonabó attacked. The Indians declared "that those who remained were well."[18] Only eleven bodies, some with their eyes extracted, were found.[19] According to the Indians, the main reason for the military confrontation was that the Spaniards had stolen the wives of the Canibas. Each Spaniard was said to have kept between three and four wives. In Caribbean society only the caciques could live in polygamy.

Caonabó's victory during the first days of November 1493 must be considered the first Indian victory, one of the few victories in the wars that finally brought about the annihilation of the Caribbean natives. In this battle, Whites fought without horses. The men and their Mestizo offspring who were not killed either escaped or were enslaved. History has forgotten these Europeans, but in reality they were the first explorers and conquerors of this strange New World.

Caribbean canoes, similar to those of Polynesia, had a capacity of up to 150 passengers.[20] They could make trips of up to 450 kilometers in the high seas; the distance from Cuba to Yucatan is only approximately 180 kilometers.[21] This was the route used by the Spanish to reach the Aztec Empire. Thus, all the stories about the existence of European chickens[22] and White people on the American mainland that were reported when Hernán Cortés came to Mexico in 1519 should not be surprising. In the same vein, all the premonitions of native soothsayers, wizards, and wise men about the destruction of the so-called high cultures of the Americas prior to the Spanish conquest must be analyzed taking into account the possibility that these Amerindians may not have been completely ignorant of the European presence in the Caribbean.[23] Long-distance trade in pre-Columbian America was intimately intertwined with shamanism. Moreover, the premonitions were reported by the Spaniards after the conquest. Columbus wrote in his journal on October 24, 1492, that there were Indian reports that large trading expeditions arrived regularly in Cuba. It is possible that these ships were from Yucatan. Since Columbus believed that Cuba was Cipango, he assumed that the merchants arriving there were from the Asian continent.[24]

A comparison of the letters, reports, and documents related to Columbus's first voyage and those of the successive voyages reveals basic differences in his descriptions of the Indians. Contrary to the documents and reports of the successive voyages, those of the first describe the Indians as a kind, honest, hard-working, and vigorous race willing to cooperate with the Whites and also to learn about the virtues of Christianity. The necessity to justify the colonization of the New World, however, produced a new type of documentation. It was during Columbus's second visit that his letters and reports described the Indians as devil worshipers, deceitful, lazy, homosexuals, prostitutes, and consumers of human flesh. During the first trip, Columbus specifically and explicitly addressed the question of whether the natives were anthropophagous. This was a question that contemporary Europeans considered very seriously about the world outside Europe. Columbus was always looking out for anthropophagous people; people with tails, single eyes, or dog faces; giants; and mermaids.[25]

Columbus noted that although the Tainos did not eat human flesh, they claimed that their enemies, the Canibas, did so. White settlers and anthropologists later discovered that this was how Amerindians slandered their local enemies. Columbus dismissed these charges. The reason the Tainos made those accusations, he thought, was that the Taino prisoners captured by the Canibas never returned and were kept as slaves.[26] Bartolomé de Las Casas categorically denies that the Canibas were anthropophagous. During Columbus's second voyage, he was able to penetrate Caniba territory and rescue Taino women and children. Apparently the Canibas were slave traders. The Canibas who survived the Spanish conquest captured their enemies and their own renegades to sell them to the British, French, and Dutch in the Windward Islands.[27] The historical evidence that the Canibas were anthropophagous is circumstantial only, and in the judgment of the American anthropologist William Arens the claim is false.[28] It is known that during the conquest Hernán Cortés and his Spanish soldiers ate one of their own compatriots "to the last hair and bone."[29] Acts of Spanish anthropophagy have also been recorded in the course of the explorations and conquest of the southwestern United States[30] and the Andes.[31] On the basis of available written evidence, it would be unfair to conclude that the Spaniards in question were cannibals. The days of the conquest were difficult even for the victors, but it is the Canibas whom the authors of dictionaries have in mind when they write about cannibals.

Christian Spain found it necessary to justify colonization in moral terms from the very beginning. In order to obtain the wholehearted collaboration among the Indians during the first voyage, however, it was not necessary for Columbus to read aloud the Requerimiento.[32] This extraordinary royal decree provided that before conducting a military attack against the Indians, a proclamation offering them peaceful subjugation had to be read. The change of mind reported in the documents after Columbus's first voyage illustrates how colonialist history was written. After the Papal Donation of 1493, Spain legitimized its world explorations to the west of the line drawn by the pope. No other colonizing nation of the American continent legitimized its authority with the pretext of converting Indians to Christianity. Only Spain proclaimed that the Indians were vassals of the king; that meant the loss of political and religious freedom for the Indians. The official attitude of the other European powers was that they were determined to control the land, which supposedly was misused by the natives.[33] In 1503, when the Spanish crown decreed that only anthropophagous people could be enslaved, it condemned the Aztecs to the fantasy of being cannibals even before they were discovered. The famous Spanish chronicler Bernal Díaz del Castillo informs us that in Montezuma's palace, more than thirty types of meats were eaten, and none of them were human flesh.[34]

When Cortés and his followers arrived at the island of Cozumel in February 1519, they were welcomed in loud voices by the natives as Castellanos, not as gods. It was the first time that the Indians of Mexico had witnessed such a large White expedition on their sovereign territory. The expeditionary force of Cortés included 550 Spaniards and 200 Cuban Indians.[35] They were veterans of the pacification campaigns against the Cuban Indians. In addition, two Yucatan Indians, Julianillo and Melchorejo, served as guides and translators. Writers have assumed that they had been captured by a previous Spanish expedition. The relations between Cortés and the natives of Cozumel were generally cordial, and there was a voluntary exchange of all kinds of merchandise. The Indians of Cozumel were of Mayan stock. In spite of all the supposed Mayan decadence, these Amerin-

dians had the most developed merchant class in the Americas at
the time of the Spanish conquest.[36] Among the Aztec merchants
(Pochteca) and Incas (Mindala), there were great entrepreneurs, but
only among the Mayas (Polóm) and the Chinchas[37] were there merchant kings in the times of the Spanish conquest.

While he was in Cozumel, Cortés was informed by the natives that
several Spaniards were living on the Mexican mainland.[38] Cortés was
able to buy the freedom of the Spaniard Jerónimo de Aguilar, who was
being held as a slave by the natives of Yucatan. De Aguilar told Cortés
that there were more Spaniards farther inland. According to the
Spanish chronicles, De Aguilar and his countryman Gonzalo Guerrero
had been stranded in Yucatan after a shipwreck in 1511. De Aguilar
and Guerrero arrived together with fifteen Spanish men and two Spanish women when they trafficked in precious metals in the Castilla
del Oro (Panama)-Hispaniola route. Guerrero had been assimilated
into the local society as a noble, and had built a family. He refused to
be rescued by Cortés. In 1535, Guerrero died fighting against the
Spanish in defense of Chectemal, the religious and intellectual center
as well as the site of a major library in Yucatan. As for the other
Spaniards, De Aguilar informed Cortés that they were too dispersed
to be rounded up.

In 1518, when the Spaniard Juan de Grijalva explored the eastern
Mexican coast, he met a Jamaican woman who together with ten of
her countrymen had come to Mexico two years earlier.[39] Western
writers presume that the Jamaicans were stranded after a sea voyage.
This attitude, in reality, reflects these writers' prejudices rather than
the facts about the discovery and conquest. Before Cortés discovered
Mexico, the Caribbean islands certainly were not totally isolated from
the Mexican mainland. The intermediary zones between the already
established European colonization and those that still remained
under Indian control were permeable. Those regions were not always
involved in armed conflict, and from the very beginning there were
peaceful incursions into each other's territories by both Whites and
Indians.

After hiring De Aguilar as an interpreter and guide, Cortés led his
expedition to the area of present-day Veracruz. In eastern Mexico,

Cortés befriended the critics and enemies of the Aztec emperor Montezuma. Cortés conducted a friendly and profitable trade with the natives of the region, and whenever some Spanish soldiers forcefully took advantage of the Indians, he intervened in favor of the natives. Cortés, like Francisco Pizarro, would penetrate the new frontiers with the stated intention of correcting and compensating for abuses by previous intruders. On March 12, 1519, during the time of Cortés's friendly exploration and trade with the ethnic chiefdoms in eastern Mexico, he was given twenty young women. One of them was Malintzin (Malinche), who was fluent in Mayan and Nahua. De Aguilar and Malintzin would prove most useful to Cortés in the beginning of the conquering enterprise. Both became his translators and servants, and Malintzin eventually became his mistress, although he later abandoned her.

Meanwhile, Cortés sent a message to Montezuma asking for permission to visit Tenochtitlán and to bring greetings from Charles V, Cortés's king. Cortés also placed himself at the service of the Aztec emperor.[40] The response from Montezuma was diplomatically polite. The emperor informed Cortés that, although he was happy for the visit, he was too busy to grant Cortés an appointment. Quinto Albor (The Fifth Brightness), an Aztec military officer of European appearance, delivered the message as well as gifts. Quinto Albor had a remarkable physical similarity to Cortés himself.[41] The Spanish chroniclers noted that Montezuma kept white-looking people as servants and retainers. Modern scholars have assumed that they were albino Indians. Such an assumption ignores the existence in the area of shipwrecked European sailors as well as freelance explorers from the very outset of the colonization process. The history of White-Indian relations begins with the first physical contact they made, and not with Spanish royal grants to famous conquistadores.

Much ink and paper has been used by Western writers to explain the speed of the Spanish conquest in terms of the Indian belief that Whites were gods riding on ferocious beasts and shooting thunder. In great part, this misconception is the result of their ignorance about the existence of social classes among the Indians. An analysis of the way in which various social strata experienced the Spanish conquest will help to revise many strange theories. From the very beginning, most Indians treated Whites with reverence, but they also treated their own lords and masters in the same manner. The Indians saluted and gave presents to Spanish soldiers according to their rank and class. The fact that two Whites, Jerónimo De Aguilar and Gonzalo Guerrero, came eight years before Cortés to Yucatan and became assimilated, the first as a slave and the latter as a noble, shows that being White did not automatically guarantee treatment as a lord or god. The Peruvian historian Pablo Macera writes that when the Inca emperor Atahualpa was under Spanish custody, "he behaved as a prince and had social contempt for the Spaniards who were not of noble birth."[42] From the very beginning, the Indians realized that the Whites were not divine and that their horses were not demons. Certainly there were stories among the Amerindians about visitors "from the other side of the sea" before the Spanish arrival. Those voyagers probably came from Asia.[43] The story of the Indian belief that the Whites were gods from Europe emerges after the Spanish conquest under the auspices of colonialist historiography.[44]

When Cortés eventually arrived at Tenochtitlán, he was cordially welcomed as a guest of honor. The Spaniards remained 235 days in the Aztec capital before they were expelled and defeated in the famous Night of Sorrows (June 30, 1520). More than one thousand Indian allies of Cortés died as well as 860 Spanish soldiers and five Spanish women. But in the beginning, the relations between Spaniards and Aztecs were friendly. For almost a week, the Spaniards were taken on tours, wined and dined by the Aztec hosts in their capital. On the sixth or seventh day, Cortés and five elite soldiers kidnapped the Aztec monarch at sword-point in the midst of a friendly conversation.[45] The emperor was completely surprised. Obviously, he never thought that such a thing could ever happen to him. It was a palace coup, and in the beginning not even the highest officials of the state apparatus realized that Montezuma had lost control of his empire. The lower classes were even less aware of the change in power. What was obvious was that Montezuma had a new palace guard. Moreover, Montezuma enjoyed the company of a blond youngster, Juan Ortega (Orteguilla). At their first encounter, Orteguilla became the apple of Montezuma's eye. Cortés gave Orteguilla to the emperor as a servant to comb, bathe, and assist him with other personal needs. Orteguilla became Montezuma's page as well as a spy in the service of Cortés.

A revolt against the state and the Spanish did not begin until it became clear to the Aztec masses that those soldiers following the emperor everywhere were in fact controlling him. According to the Códice Florentino compiled by Aztec informers immediately after the conquest, before the Aztecs became enemies of the Spaniards, "we were their friends for 195 days."[46] Although initially the Aztecs defeated Cortés in battle, his soldiers infected the victorious natives with smallpox. In the following year (1520–21), almost forty percent of the population in the Mexican Central Valley died from European plagues. The conquest of the Americas was also a war of microbes in which the Europeans were favored.

When the Spaniards kidnapped Montezuma, he was about forty years old, was married, and had several concubines as well as sons and daughters. Montezuma was of delicate physique and had the manners of a prince. Perhaps somewhat effeminate, he was melancholic and often cried. His nephew Cacamatzin considered the emperor to be as brave as a chicken.[47] The chronicler Díaz del Castillo, who admired Montezuma, exonerates him from having any "unnatural vices."[48] Montezuma informed Cortés that Cacamatzin was leading a conspiracy against the Spaniards. In addition, he collaborated with the Spaniards in the kidnapping of his nephew. Both would die when the Spanish escaped in the catastrophe of the Night of Sorrows. Orteguilla also died during the Spanish retreat. The historian Ross Hassig concludes that Montezuma was not a coward, but he was afraid to lose his political power in Aztec society.[49]

Despite his initial hesitation, Montezuma became enchanted with the Spanish visitors from the first encounter. His previous irresolution was due to the fact that his court was not sure whether Cortés really was the official representative of a great king or only a common adventurer.[50] Although they are biased, some Spanish reports tell of conversations between Cortés and Montezuma before and after Montezuma was made prisoner. As a host the emperor was most inquisitive about Cortés's homeland, his religion, and, in particular, Spanish weapons. When the mystery of the Holy Trinity was explained to Montezuma, he concluded that the Christian gods must be the same as the Aztec gods because both were "good and fair."[51] Montezuma vainly proposed that the Cross and the Christian saints be placed side by side in the Aztec altars.[52] During these conversations, Montezuma noted that his subjects had informed him about the magical European guns that produced thunder and lightning, but that after examining them, he had found that these guns were made on the same principle as native blowguns. As for the Spanish swords, he had already received one as a gift from one of his own Indian vassals. Montezuma did not see anything ferocious about the horses, and he thought they were a type of deer.[53] Similarly, before the Inca emperor Atahualpa was kidnapped, he was visited by Hernando de Soto and Hernando Pizarro together with their cavalry. During a show of horsemanship in which the animals were nearly foaming over the Peruvian monarch, he did not even move an eyebrow or show any fear.[54]

Horses were feared not because they were thought to be ferocious demons, but because, in military terms, they had the advantage of being strong and fast. Horses have been perceptively called by commentators on the conquest the "tanks of the conquest," and the Indians were quick to adopt them in battle. Manco Inca, half brother of Atahualpa and the Spaniards' puppet emperor, conducted his final revolt against the Spanish on horseback and with European weapons, together with a platoon of native cavalry. His army even produced gunpowder in its resistance against the invaders. Moreover, the Indians of Patagonia and those of the southwestern United States became skillful horsemen before they ever met the White man. Unfortunately for the Amerindians, horses by then had lost much of their strategic value, for the White man had added other factors to the invasion and domination of the Americas.

With respect to the myth that Montezuma thought that Whites were gods, written sources show the contrary.[55] The Aztec emperor revealed to Cortés that he was of human flesh just like the visitors themselves, and he allowed the Spanish conqueror to touch his hands and body to verify this. However, Montezuma noted that most people thought of him as divine. It is documented that no common Indian was permitted to look Montezuma straight in the eye. Much evidence does suggest that the Spaniards pretended to believe that the emperors Montezuma and Atahualpa were divine so that the Indians would let the Spaniards come near them. Montezuma had an escort of two hundred noblemen. The Inca emperors proclaimed themselves divine and sons of the sun. Hernando de Soto, after his participation in the Peruvian conquest, organized an expedition of the North American southeast, proclaiming to be the son of the sun. However, when he met Chief Quigaltan of the Natchez, Quigaltan told him that before he believed such a thing, de Soto must first dry up the waters of the Mississippi River.[56]

Strategy in the conquest of the New World changed with the advancement of the White frontier, but from the very outset the kidnapping of native chiefs by *baquianos* (gangs of conquistadores) was the main characteristic. White adventurers, pretending to come as friends or for the purpose of trading for mutual benefit, usually penetrated Indian communities. The Spaniards were loaded with "diamonds" and "emeralds" made of glass, which they brought for barter and as gifts. Since the Europeans were few in number, the Indians underestimated the danger they posed. Once the visitors gained the confidence and trust of the natives, they would surprise them by taking their leaders as hostages. This strategy applied to the capture of Guacanagarí and Caonabó in the Caribbean as well as that of the emperors Montezuma and Atahualpa in Mexico and Peru. The systematic capture of hostages was continued after the first hostages had been taken. They were then used as bait to capture other important native figures. However, during the conquest, the Indians as well as the Europeans captured hostages in order to exchange them for war booty. In the case of the Indians, it was to exchange them for their own captives or to keep them as souvenirs.

The practice of kidnapping was not limited to military or political operations; Catholic clergy used it to bring about the massive conversion of natives. The usual procedure involved kidnapping the children of the native elites in order to indoctrinate them and keep them as interns in schools operated by the church. After these children were considered thoroughly indoctrinated, they were released for the purpose of converting their compatriots of humbler birth.[57] The indoctrinated children and young men denounced and persecuted the practitioners of native religions. With perverse cruelty, in the name of the Christian God, the native priesthood was brutally persecuted and extirpated. It was a struggle against paganism with all its aberrations. The native priests and priestess were subjected to forced labor, torture, and being burned alive. The friar Diego de Landa not only incinerated Mayan libraries and manuscripts, but literally destroyed Chectemal, Yucatan's intellectual city. In the Christian expansion, the conquerors tolerated no theological debate by Amerindian priests. De Landa considered the scholarly activity of Chectemal at the Salamanca University to be in the service of the devil. The native temples and worship centers were quickly destroyed, and with the same stones and in the same places, churches were built with the labor of the neophyte Christians. In addition, the extirpation of idolatries included the confiscation of individual property from the accused Indians.[58]

Wherever Amerindian deities and spiritual symbols existed, the Catholic Church approved and confirmed the appearance of saints and virgins. Such a prototype of colonial political expediency and religious syncretism is clearly illustrated by the appearance of the Virgin of Guadalupe (1531) in the same place where the Mexican Indians worshiped the mother goddess Tonantzin. Her believers and Catholic bureaucrats continue to verify old miracles to this day. Tonantzin, however, like other Amerindian goddesses, was generally connected to Mother Earth and fertility cults. Gradually Catholic virgins and saints were substituted for the Amerindian goddesses as the colonizing process advanced. Although the Catholic Church was successful in implanting Christianity in Latin America, it failed to eliminate the practices and cults of Amerindian and African religions. Those syncretisms have subsisted until today, not only in Indian and Black communities, but among mixed populations, and even among a few Whites. The Señor de los Milagros (Lord of Miracles) originated with the Peruvian Lord of Pachacamac (Mover of the Universe). This cult, started by Indians, was eventually followed by Blacks and continued by criollos. Among the African religions, the Yoruba cults had the greatest impact in Latin America. Moreover, Brazilian Indians adopted the Yoruba cosmology of the Caboclo in their religion.[59]

Latin American syncretism has survived despite persecution by the Catholic Church as well as the colonial and the postcolonial state. The Bishop Manuel Abad y Queipo (1751–1825), who spent almost all his life evangelizing and fighting heresies among Mexican Indians, noted: "Each Indian community secretly supports from eight to ten lazy and superstitious old men, who dominate the Indians with the most despotic and unbelievable cruelty."[60] Shamans cured sicknesses and guided the Amerindians through their spiritual world. Before the Aztecs were defeated, smallpox epidemics had invaded Tenochtitlán. In the same way, before the Spanish invaded Peru, European pests had already killed the highest Incan cadres. The failure and disgrace of the shamans to cure the unknown plagues was seen as a defeat for the Amerindian gods.

Another crucial aspect of the Spanish conquest consisted of the alliances made between conquistadores and the local ethnic enemies. When the besieged Aztecs finally surrendered their capital city on August 13, 1521, the armies of Cortés included more than 150,000 Indians (most of them from Tlaxcala) and only 900 Spaniards.[61] Indeed, more Tlaxcalans than Spaniards felt themselves victorious, but for them, it was a short-lived victory in which native ethnic groups killed each other. The Tlaxcalans would help the Spanish in the subjugation and colonization of the Mexican northwest (Chichimecs), Central America, and even Peru. Local ethnic conflicts were of extreme importance in the European victory and domination process. Although the Indian partners of the Spanish have been considered to be mere auxiliaries, many of them were trained and strategically led by Spanish officers. Some of them used European weapons, and above all, they knew the terrain. Regardless of how insignificant the role of the Indian auxiliaries was in the victory over the Aztecs, more Indians than Spaniards had the feeling that the victory was theirs. The alliance against the Aztecs was concluded through the marriage of five Spanish captains with Tlaxcalan princesses as well as three hundred Spanish soldiers to young plebeian women of the same ethnic group. But when European women came to Mexico, many of those native wives were replaced or downgraded. At first, however, the Tlaxcalans believed that they had made a fraternal and blood pact with the conquistadores.

After Columbus's fourth voyage (1502–1504), the Spanish would follow what was called the "golden" route and a passage to the other side of Panamanian isthmus (Ver-Aguas). New gangs of adventurers landed on the Caribbean coast of Panama (Golden Castile). The Spanish conquest of Panama was gradually achieved by adventurers and shipwrecked sailors, who traded and made alliances with the native chiefs or caciques. By 1510, the caciques, Comagre and Panquiaco, confirmed to Vasco Núñez de Balboa that from the western side of the isthmus it was possible to reach the golden realm of the Incas. The Spanish fantasies increased even more. But, before Balboa could discover the Pacific Ocean, he had to ask for permission from the cacique Chima, who controlled Careta (the western coast of Panama).

The conquest of the Inca Empire actually begins with the discovery of the Pacific Ocean by Balboa in 1513. From the outset, freelance explorers, adventurers, and vagabonds visited the western coasts of South America and the adjacent islands. According to the Mestizo chronicler Blas de Valera, a Spanish ship reached the Virú River in northern Peru only three years after Balboa's first incursion into the Pacific. The inability of the conquistadores to pronounce the name Virú resulted in the name Peru for the ancient Inca lands.[62] A decade later, Sebastián de Guevara explored the western coast of South America from the Strait of Magellan to Nicaragua.[63] Before Francisco Pizarro invaded the Inca Empire, several Spaniards lived on the Peruvian coast and the adjacent islands; we know only a few of their names or surnames, such as Bocanegra, Ginés, and Alonso de Molina.[64] When Pizarro arrived at the northern Peruvian coast in early 1532, he found more than thirty Mestizo boys and girls living on the island of Puná. These children were the offspring of Spanish men and Indian women.[65] Pizarro also brought two Peruvian interpreters, Felipillo and Martinillo, who spoke fluent Spanish and had already visited

Spain. It is likely that Martinillo was the first Peruvian to bring with him a Spanish wife. Martinillo later became an *encomendero* and was rewarded with the title of Knight by the Spanish king.[66]

After Balboa was executed by the Panamanian governor and money-lender Pedro Arias Dávila (Pedrarias) in 1519, Pizarro emerged as the major entrepreneur of expeditions to South America. Pizarro was second-in-command to Balboa as well as his supposedly loyal friend. Pizarro arrested Balboa by orders of Pedrarias in order to execute him. It should be noted that apart from Cortés's expedition, all the Spanish conquests of America were legally authorized by the crown. In the conquering process, a feasible plan had to be approved first. The discoverers and conquerors whom history has recognized were those who kept official papers that legitimized their deeds and inheritances. Only the newly acquired wealth of Cortés and Pizarro made it possible for the crown to cancel the discovery of Mexico by Diego Velásquez[67] and of Peru by Pedrarias.

The traditional accounts of the Spanish conquest overemphasize the fighting skills of the famous conquistadores. In fact, most of them were past their prime for hand-to-hand combat. For example, when Pizarro arrived at Cajamarca he was already nearly fifty-five years old. Indeed, the narratives of the conquest closely resemble medieval European tales of chivalry.

Although only 168 Spaniards participated in the capture of Atahualpa, records indicate that Pizarro's expedition included hundreds of Nicaraguan auxiliaries.[68] The use of natives was of strategic military significance. Their lives were the most expendable part of the conquering enterprise but their knowledge of the local geography and native idiosyncrasies was indispensable.

When Pizarro landed for the last time in the Inca Empire during early 1532, he encountered it in the midst of a violent civil war. After the death of Emperor Huayna Capac (1493–1527) in a smallpox and measles epidemic five years earlier,[69] the empire had been shaken by the dispute between rival candidates from Quito and Cuzco. On his deathbed, the emperor had chosen his son Ninan Cayuchi as his successor, but the new heir also died almost immediately from a European plague. European epidemics gradually would accomplish what the Spanish kidnappings and firearms had not. The sudden death of Ninan Cayuchi precipitated the fratricidal war for the Incan throne. The quarreling half brothers Atahualpa and Huascar were sons of two of Huayna Capac's wives. This situation was most advantageous to the Spaniards. Historians agree that if the Tawantinsuyo had been ruled by Huayna Capac at the time of the Spanish invasion, it would have been impossible for Pizarro to conquer the Inca Empire. During the rule of Huayna Capac, the Portuguese adventurer Aleixo Garcia, allied with Guaraní Indians, already had unsuccessfully attempted to penetrate the eastern border of the Inca Empire (1524–25).[70] The Spanish invasion of Peru could have begun only after the death of Huayna Capac.

The question of why the Spanish did not attempt the conquest of the Tawantinsuyo at an earlier date, when it was still united, demands greater research. It is also not clear why it took almost three decades for the Spanish to arrive in Mexico although it took Columbus only thirty days to travel from Europe to the Caribbean. Neither Cortés nor Pizarro were the first to discover Mexico or Peru. How did the Cortés and Pizarro families legally develop the entrepreneurial capacity to conquer both empires? The documents that could identify other historical processes and personalities involved in the discovery and conquest have disappeared, and this disappearance was not completely unintentional. In any case, the Spanish invasion of the American mainland (*tierra firme*) coincided with the decline of gold production in the Caribbean. Gold fever created the opportunity for audacious Spaniards of every class to become conquistadores as well as fabulously wealthy.

The civil war among the Incas permitted the landing of Pizarro and his troops on the northern Peruvian coast almost without Indian interference. Once Pizarro found himself on the Peruvian mainland, he received messengers from both Huascar and Atahualpa asking him to come and visit them in the highlands.[71] A general of Huascar, Guaman Malqui, welcomed Pizarro in Tumbes. Since Atahualpa was nearby in Cajamarca, Pizarro accepted that invitation. The Spanish came to Cajamarca completely unobstructed. Moreover, they were lodged and fed at the royal quarters located along the route to Cajamarca. In that city, Spaniards were officially housed in one of the

royal palaces, and they met high-ranking Incan bureaucrats.[72] Cajamarca (Cusimango) had been violently conquered by the Incas in the
mid-1470s. Certainly, the Cajamarca ethnic differences with the Incas
facilitated their collaboration with the Spanish against the Incas. It is
not clear how long after his arrival at Cajamarca Francisco Pizarro
was granted an appointment with the emperor. Cajamarca was a holy
city with medicinal hot springs, and Atahualpa was relaxing and med-
itating in the nearby bathing facilities. Delegations headed by Hernando de Soto and Pizarro's brother Hernando visited Atahualpa in
friendship, and during the cordial receptions, Spaniards and Indians
drank the native corn beer together. The delegations brought greetings from the Spanish monarch, and the Spaniards placed themselves
at the service of Atahualpa for his military campaigns.[73] The Inca
emperor granted one more appointment to the Spaniard Lorenzo de
Aldana before Atahualpa and his royal entourage visited the Spaniards
in one of his Cajamarca palaces.

Traditional accounts maintain that the Spanish arrived at Cajamarca on November 15, 1532, and that Atahualpa rushed to meet
Pizarro on the very next day. They also state that it was not until the
emperor cast away the Bible, refusing to accept Christianity, that the
Spanish attacked.[74] Much effort has been spent to determine whether
the friar Vicente de Valverde was properly understood by Atahualpa.
In reality, there is much evidence to support the assertion that this
often-repeated dialogue, as described in Western historiography, never occurred. This scenario has all the trappings of official history.
Peruvian chronicler and iconographer Guaman Poma (1534–1615)
portrays Pizarro on his knees before the Inca emperor. The kidnapping of Atahualpa would not be as peaceful as that of Montezuma.
Pizarro was wounded while he protected the emperor from being
killed in the tumultuous kidnapping attack. By the time of Atahualpa's
capture, Spain had already had a moral and ethical debate on the fairness of subduing Indians without just cause. The observance of the
Requerimiento and so-called just wars were official policies of
Catholic Spain. It is very unlikely that Atahualpa would have been
motivated to meet Pizarro and his emissaries so often in such a short
time. Pizarro's presence in Cajamarca did not have the first priority

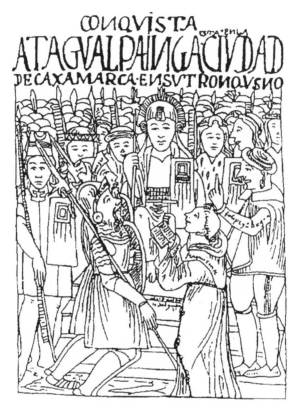

Francisco Pizarro on his knees before Atahualpa.
Is he pledging loyalty to the Inca emperor?

on the emperor's agenda.

No doubt Atahualpa and Montezuma were the victims of sweet talk and pretended loyalty; they were caught off guard and were captured in a well-planned false demonstration of loyalty. Moreover, Atahualpa, in his powerful arrogance, allowed the Spaniards to come too near him. The great similarity between the kidnappings of Atahualpa and Montezuma seems to imply that the cousins Cortés and Pizarro might have planned together the invasion of the Inca Empire. There are no documents to support this theory, but it is known that Cortés recommended Pizarro so that he would be well received by the Spanish courtiers, and that he helped Pizarro recruit competent soldiers.

A member of the Pizarro family participated in the conquest of Mexico. Pedro de Alvarado, the most loyal of Cortés's partners, refrained from assisting Pizarro only after he was given a great remuneration in gold and silver. After Cortés conquered the Aztecs, he met Pizarro at the Rábida Monastery (Moguer, Spain) in 1529.[75] Even without a joint plan for the conquest of the Incas, by then, there was already a Spanish conquering culture in the Iberian ports and towns as well as in the colonized areas where strategies, tactics, and information were exchanged about conquering enterprises. At least one of the Spaniards who participated in the defeat of the Aztecs participated in the kidnapping of Atahualpa. Pedro Pizarro, the secretary and cousin of Francisco Pizarro, while not intending to deny the official version of Atahualpa's capture, wrote that when Atahualpa was assaulted, the Lord of Chincha accompanied him. The Spaniards did not really know which of them was to be captured.[76] In the tumult of the kidnapping, the Lord of Chincha was killed. The version by Pedro Pizarro creates doubt about the official account of Atahualpa's capture. Moreover, all the recruits of conquering expeditions had to swear before it took place as to what and how a conquest was to be made. The directors of conquering expeditions had to protect their royal grants from future suits by the crown and by usurpers.

The entrepreneurial friar Valverde was supposedly the only Spaniard who participated in Atahualpa's capture, and yet he was not compensated for his fateful intervention. The encounter between Pizarro and Atahualpa occurred in a festive and musical atmosphere in which the Cajamarca Indians were singing in unison.[77] There were dancers and musicians in Atahualpa's entourage. There is also confusion among the Spanish cronistas as to whether Felipillo or Martinillo was the translator of Valverde's dialogue with the Inca emperor. Moreover, in a recently discovered and lengthy letter written immediately after Atahualpa's capture by a soldier who participated in this event, nothing is mentioned about Valverde's dialogue.[78] It would be a historical irony if so much had been written and read about an event that never took place. It is clear that the so-called Spanish humanism of the sixteenth century demanded some formalities when new vassals were subjected.

After their capture, both Atahualpa and Montezuma were allowed a number of privileges in exchange for their collaboration. They continued to perform ceremonial rites of power. In their luxurious imprisonment both were taught a number of European card games as well as chess. Atahualpa learned Spanish in only twenty days; Spanish chroniclers were full of praise about the wisdom and intelligence of the two distinguished prisoners. But the usefulness of these hostages was dictated by the priorities of the Spanish conquest. The Spanish chronicles claim that Montezuma was killed by a stone thrown by Aztec crowds when he tried to address them, but Indian chroniclers write that Spaniards strangled Montezuma. In the case of Atahualpa, the Spaniards wanted to obtain as much treasure as possible, but their main intention was to capture Cuzco easily. The ransom extorted from Atahualpa amounted to 6,087 kilograms in gold and 11,793 kilograms in silver.[79] From the very beginning, Atahualpa's fate was subject to Spanish negotiations with his enemies. Just as Cortés allied himself with the Tlaxcalans against the Aztecs, Pizarro received enthusiastic support from the Cañaris, Huancas, and Chachapuyas. According to the traditional historiography, Atahualpa was strangled by Spaniards, but the Indian chronicler Guaman Poma describes his execution as a beheading. The emperor was killed on July 26, 1533. Approximately three months later, the Spaniards and Atahualpa's half brother Manco Inca entered the Tawantinsuyo's capital as allies. After over a month of celebrations in which Spaniards and natives fraternized with the help of chicha and coca, the Tawantinsuyo had a new emperor. Manco Inca enthusiastically granted generous privileges to his foreign allies, who ostensibly were helping him to pacify his empire. Not until March 23, 1534, did Manco Inca lose the sovereignty of his capital, when Cuzco was reorganized as a Spanish city.

Manco Inca was urinated upon and humiliated in the worst manner; his wife Cura Ocllo was raped and murdered in his presence. Obviously, this was not what Manco Inca had anticipated when he allied himself with the Spanish conquerors. A conspiracy was formulated against the Spanish and their Indian collaborators. By May 1536, Cuzco was besieged by Manco Inca's armies. Ironically, the beleaguered Spaniards were well provided with food and supplies from

Cuzco's royal depositories. The siege lasted for nearly a year. The Spanish were attacked throughout the Inca Empire, but reinforcements from the other Spanish colonies and Spain itself saved the White colonization of Peru. Moreover, the besiegers, following the Incan agricultural tradition, retreated in order to collect their harvests. Like the Mesoamerican warriors, the Andeans fought according to the agricultural calendar. The Spanish chroniclers considered this interregnum a miraculous period in which the Virgin Mary and the apostle Santiago appeared in the skies to save Christianity in the Andes. It has been estimated that about two thousand Spaniards died as result of this Indian revolt.[80]

Manco Inca's inability to force the Spanish to surrender caused him to retreat to Vilcabamba, to the northwest of the imperial capital. For nearly four decades, Manco Inca and his descendants operated a Neo-Inca state outside Spanish control. Vilcabamba also became a sanctuary for Indians escaping from the Spaniards, and a base from which to launch guerrilla attacks. After a measles epidemic in Vilcabamba, a military expedition of 250 Spaniards and 1,500 Cañari Indians penetrated the Neo-Inca state in 1572.[81] The Cañaris were the first Gurkha (mercenary) soldiers of the Inca Empire under Spanish rule. The Spanish had gained the collaboration of the treacherous Puma Inca, one of the captains of the last Inca emperor, Tupac Amaru. The monarch managed to escape but was persuaded to surrender through many promises by two Mestizo soldiers, Francisco de la Peña and Chávez Amaru, who were working for the Spanish army.[82] On this occasion, the Spanish authorities decided to drop the pretense of ruling through a native monarch. This was a time when the private entrepreneurial conquest was yielding authority to the bureaucracy of the colonial state. Tupac Amaru was executed on September 24, 1572. As a result of the death of the last Inca monarch, Spain had finally gained complete control of its richest colony. This would be true until 1670, when Mexico would definitely lead in the production of precious metals.

One of the most puzzling aspects of the Spanish conquest is the fact that very small numbers of Whites were able to subdue large Indian masses. Although the Whites possessed superior military technology, this is only one of several important factors. In any analysis of the Spanish conquest, the role of White-Indian alliances in the battles against other Indian ethnic groups should by no means be underrated. From the outset, various native ethnic groups were in the forefront of the Spanish conquering process. Western historians have emphasized the European military superiority, but the conquest had an important political aspect that cannot be minimized. Father Las Casas described the Indians as extremely political people. Europeans and Indians not only fought each other; from the outset, they also negotiated. However, political considerations were valid only in the short term. Unlike the conquistadores, who had a global strategy of subjugating all the natives, the Amerindians gave priority to their own ethnic groups and regions. The Amerindians still did not understand that for the Whites, all the native nobles, monarchs, and ethnic groups had been reduced to one people, Indians.

Unfortunately, many well-meaning Western scholars, in their efforts to portray the Indians as noble savages, have forgotten to consider the human qualities and socioeconomic conflicts that made the Indians collaborators with the Spanish and even traitors to their own people. Indians, like other peoples in other parts of the planet, were victims of their own economic, political, ethnic, and regional conflicts.

With the passing of time, as the Europeans developed a more autonomous power base in which their security was more closely linked to the colonial metropolis than to their native collaborators, the former native allies were subjected to many of the same cruelties that had been applied to the fiercest native enemies.[83] Even the Mestizos were abandoned with the Westernization of the New World. Throughout the Americas, the meager numbers of White invaders deceived the more numerous natives and made them overconfident about their security until it was too late. Wave after wave of new European arrivals indicated that Europe had reached a new age of expansion. This experience was novel to both Indians and Europeans. Until the eighteenth century the European powers would continue to seek political and military alliances with various Indian nations in order to promote their colonial projects or confront their European competitors.

The "discovery of America" coincides with a long-term process that started in the fifteenth century with the expansion of European colonialism outside the European continent. In this macrohistorical process, the only non-Whites who escaped defeat were the Japanese. The underdevelopment of the so-called Third World is intimately intertwined with the supremacy of the White man after the fifteenth century. Other developments and processes might have flourished if the peoples of the Third World had more to say about the manner in which it related to the Europeans and Christianity from the beginning. The Amerindians reacted and adjusted militarily and politically against the European invasion, but the Whites increased their power at a faster rate. At the time of the Spanish conquest, the misfortune of the Indians was that they had gold and silver. The existence of precious metals motivated and mobilized the most unlikely individuals to become conquistadores. In a sense, the conquest has not yet come to an end, because Indians still live in lands where gold, oil, uranium, and even good soils for coca cultivation can be found. There is no doubt that the native owners of these resources will eventually be "civilized."

It has been claimed that the more civilized the Indians were, the easier it was to conquer them. This abstraction contains a high level of truth, but it also undermines the importance of the struggle for survival of the supposedly less civilized Indians under the domination of powerful native states and, later on, their efforts of adjustment to European colonialism.[84] It is more a question of how absolutist each native state was than of how civilized the Indians were. The Araucanians resisted until 1883. Perhaps the most civilized and least militaristic Amerindians were the Mayas, but they were the most difficult for the White invaders to subdue either politically or militarily. The last center of Mayan resistance was finally defeated in 1697. Later, in the Caste War (1847), the Mayas made another attempt to expel the Whites from their territories. The Lacandoneans of Mayan stock were able to survive until modern times only by fleeing to the Chiapas jungle. Unlike the Incas and the Aztecs, the Mayas did not form a powerful and centralized state apparatus. The Mayan model of political organization was similar to that of the city-states of Greek antiquity. Much of the Caniba success in resisting European attacks was due to the fact that their chiefs were popularly elected. When Caniba leaders were kidnapped, their societies were not immobilized. New leaders were immediately elected.[85]

The ethnic groups of the marginal regions where there was no gold had a better opportunity of resisting the European offensive, while Indians who had no place to which to escape, in an effort to maintain their dignity, committed mass suicide, practiced infanticide, and refused to have more children. Sedentary Indians like the Apaches and others, who lived on the periphery of the Spanish colonization, became nomads and fierce warriors.[86] In 1511, the cacique Hatuey and his Taino followers were burned alive because they refused to become Christians. Before his execution in Cuba, Hatuey declared plainly and with dignity that he did not wish to share the Catholic heaven with the Spaniards.

In the same spirit, some Amerindian women would neglect their physical appearance and cover their beauty with rags in order to avoid the lust of the conquistadores. During the conquest of the Mayas, when a native virgin girl refused to be raped by the Spanish captain Alfonso López de Avila, she was thrown to the Spanish dogs to be eaten.

Much has been written about the horses of the conquerors, but very little about their dogs. In the orgy of violence, the Spaniards came along with ferocious dogs (Dogo-Mastín) specially and systematically trained to attack and devour Indians.

Eventually, when the Spanish crown established a colonial legal-rights system, the Indians would become persistent litigators in the judicial courts.

Despite the overwhelming anthropological, ethnological, and archeological evidence about the existence of contacts between South American and Mesoamerican Indians, historians have acted as if those connections never existed.[87] On the Peruvian northwestern coast archeologists have excavated ceramics with Aztec symbols such as, for example, that of an eagle eating a serpent on a cactus tree.[88] Pre-Columbian South America exported metals to Mesoamerica and the Caribbean in exchange for pearls. A great variety of Andean artifacts and products have been found in archeological excavations of Central America.[89] During the time of Columbus, the Andean region even exported coca leaves to the Caribbean.[90] Moreover, some ethnic groups of the Peruvian northwest spoke languages similar to those of Mesoamerica.[91] In both regions there were toponymic similarities. It should not be surprising that Pizarro took hundreds of Nicaraguan Indians as guides and assistants. But why do the Spanish conquerors and discoverers appear as subjects and the Indians as objects in traditional historiography? Perhaps if that fact is confronted, this question arises: Why was no warning given to the Incas by the Aztecs about the Spaniards' deceitfulness? This question may appear naïve, but it is also an illustration of the unevenness of scholarship concerning the Amerindian past.

After 1513, the Panama-Nicaragua area gradually fell into Spanish hands. Before the European takeover of this region, Andean and Mesoamerican merchants used it as a trade route. The first Spanish contacts with the Tawantinsuyo in the Pacific Ocean were with sailors and merchants from Chincha. The Chinchas were legendary for their dexterity as navigators. It is not surprising that the guides, allies, and interpreters of Pizarro, Felipillo and Martinillo, were natives from Chinchaysuyo. Spanish chroniclers have recorded that in 1526, an Incan ship leaving the northern boundaries of the Empire en route to Panama was captured by the Spanish. The vessel was carrying twenty persons including passengers and crew, and it was loaded with more than thirty tons of merchandise.[92] This was surely not the only Incan boat that became a Spanish prize on this route. At the time of the Spanish conquest, Ecuadorian merchants had ships that traded with Mesoamerica, with the capacity to carry sixty passengers.[93] Regardless of how intensive the trade or how frequent the communications between South and North America were, it can be shown that these contacts were obstructed by the Spanish even before the conquest of Peru began. The Chinchas, like the Indians of coastal Ecuador and southwest Colombia, were great merchants even before they were incorporated into the Inca Empire. In exchange for exotic products, the Incas exempted those merchants from the mita.[94] One of the products most appreciated by the Incas were seashells, or *mullu* (spondylus). Mullu (food of the gods) was utilized in all the Andean religious ceremonies. Likewise, pulverized mullu helped to dissolve the coca leaves when they were chewed. The most prized mullu was found from the Gulf of California to Ecuador. The *pututo* (sonorous seashell) used by Incan musicians came from the Panamanian region. It is within this context that the trade between Mesoamerica and the northern Inca Empire must be understood. It is documented that the Indians of northern Peru continued trading with Panama in their rustic vessels until the end of the seventeenth century.[95]

After the Spanish victory in Mexico, the conquering frontier moved southward with new impetus. Even if the Aztecs had managed to convey the news of their tragic fate at Spanish hands to the highest echelons of the Incan government, it does not follow that the Incas would have responded with greater caution to overtures by Whites. We know that after Cortés had completed the conquest of the Aztecs, he launched an expedition into Mayan territory in 1525, taking as hostage and puppet the Aztec emperor Cuauhtémoc. When this expedition met the Maya king Apoxpalón, the Aztec emperor secretly informed him about the Spanish menace. Furthermore, Cuauhtémoc asked Apoxpalón to join him in a conspiracy against the Spanish, but the Maya king informed Cortés about the plot. As a result, the last Aztec emperor and his fellow conspirators were executed with the collaboration of the Maya Indians.[96] This event is not without other historical parallels during the days of the Spanish conquest.

Indian collaboration in the defeat of the Indians themselves runs through the very heart of post-Columbian Amerindian history. The Indian assistance to White supremacy survived as a subordinate partnership in the exploitation of other Indians. The indigenismo of the Americas has not yet been able to reach the high tempo of Afro-Americanism or Negritude. Perhaps the cause of this lethargy is that Whites have been more prompt to recognize the little Amerindian blood they might have than to acknowledge the Negroid blood in their veins. Descendants of the defeated Indian masses are now mostly Mestizos, but history has shown that Mestizos have preferred and hoped to become White rather than Indian. This is also a long-term process of self-annihilation.

FROM UNDERDEVELOPMENT TO NEOCOLONIALISM

At the time of the discovery of America, the economies of Spain and Portugal were beginning an unequal and dependent relationship with Western Europe. Spain exported iron, wool, wines, and raw materials to Europe. Portugal imported grains, metallurgical products, and salted fish in exchange for salt and African gold. Despite the Iberian agricultural-pastoral economy, with its precapitalist social institutions, its geography and navigational sophistication enabled the Iberians to become pioneers in establishing maritime colonies. The Portuguese and Castilians developed the caravel with sails and without oars for navigating in the high seas. The Iberian long-distance merchant trade of the fifteenth century consisted of the exchange of high-value small products. However, the massive entrance of American precious metals into Spain enabled Spain to import manufactured products at relatively cheap prices, and at the same time, ingeniously destroyed its infant industries.

Although the British economist Patrick O'Brien has verified that the contribution of the periphery to the industrial development of the metropolis has been only "peripheral,"[97] Latin American colonies, at least, subsidized the European industries and their commerce with Africa and Asia. Long-distance trade with the periphery was one of the most dynamic sectors of capitalist expansion in the metropolitan centers. Moreover, the periphery allowed Europeans to live beyond their own means. Adam Smith and Karl Marx considered the European colonial expansion of the sixteenth century to be transcendental for the development of the world economy. European growth during the sixteenth century was massive, sustained, and gen-

The first European map of Peru (top) was made in situ by Diego Méndez between 1565 and 1574. Notice the Inca ship (detail) by the Central American Pacific coast. See Raúl Porras Barrenechea, *Fuentes históricas peruanas* (Lima, 1955), 388–89.

eralized; it included all categories, prices, volumes, and exchanges. Indeed, the price revolution in the European space was influenced by the entrance of the Americas into the newly born world economic system.[98]

The expulsion of the Jews from the Iberian Peninsula at the end of the fifteenth century deprived Iberia of financial, entrepreneurial, and artisan resources, while indirectly benefiting English and Western European merchants, bankers, and industrialists. Iberia lost an entrepreneurial group that was necessary for dynamic economic development. The Spanish fleets were regularly supplied and financed by English, Genovese, Dutch, and French merchants. Although the long-distance trade of the Portuguese merchants produced great profits, those profits were not invested in the industrialization of Portugal. The Iberian society that conquered the Americas and the world was strictly feudal, and the political economy was dominated by the ruling elites of that feudal society. The relations of production and level of Iberian economic development would have profound consequences in the evolution of the overseas empires, especially in Latin America.

The Latin American colonies paid for their own administration and gave fiscal profits to the metropolitan centers. During the great Spanish American mining boom (1545–1610), private enterprise, with state collaboration, exploited the mines and shared the profits. The payment of the Royal Fifth was an obligatory requirement for the operation of mines. Approximately forty percent of all precious metals entering Spain constituted government income. It included the Royal Fifth and other taxes, among which were the Indian tribute; the royal monopolies in mercury, gunpowder, salt, playing cards, stamped paper; ecclesiastical tithes (of which 9 percent was for the royal treasury), indulgences, and contributions for crusades. The rest of the gold and silver went into private hands. In the early nineteenth century, the Prussian savant Alexander von Humboldt calculated that from 1493 to 1803, the Ibero-American mines had produced 5,706,700,000 pesos in gold and silver.

The key products of mercantilist and imperial concern were precious metals, but agriculture and cattle-raising would become more

Alliances and wars of the conquest between Indians and whites
according to the Indian chronicler Guaman Poma (1534–1615).

important for the Iberian American economy. The ideology of mercantilist imperialism was that the colonies should produce raw materials or products needed in the metropolis, and the colonies should
serve as a market for metropolitan goods. The Spanish American
colonies partly played such a role during the sixteenth century, when
tanned skins, dyes, and precious metals entered Spain in exchange for
metropolitan products. Gradually, the economies of the New World
and Spain began to compete with each other. By the end of the sixteenth century, both regions were producing practically the same
items. Textiles, grains, and other agricultural products of European origin were already produced in the colonies. When the duplication of
Spanish and Spanish American production took place, it was decided
that direct contact between Mexico, Peru, and the Philippines would
be limited. Without too much success, the crown tried to eliminate
the export of precious metals, especially to Asia. In reality, the Chinese
merchants had opened shop in Manila in order to absorb Spanish
American silver. Manila became the "Asian Venice" for the emergent
Spanish and Spanish American commercial elite. Despite imperial

prohibitions and punishments, in Manila everything was bought and sold, legally or otherwise. Although most of the precious metals went to Europe, eight thousand tons of silver entered annually into China through Manila by the beginning of the seventeenth century.[99]

By the end of the seventeenth century, England had experienced great political and economic changes that increased its supremacy over the Iberian world. Unlike the Iberians, English landowners and merchants together invested in overseas enterprises through shareholding companies from the sixteenth century onward. There is consensus that English industrialization originated mostly because of internal changes in the relations of production, manufacture, and commerce. The emergence of an agricultural revolution, technological advances, banking institutions, and companies with limited liability reinforced British capacity for production. In addition, the merchant elite gradually came to predominate in parliamentary decisions.

By the end of the seventeenth century, England had overcome its position as mere exporter of raw materials. In exchange for gold and silver, the country was already exporting textiles to the Iberian peninsula, which were reexported to the colonies. Spain and Portugal did not have the capacity to supply their colonies with textiles and metallurgical goods or the means to pay for their imports without colonial products. Their system gave profits to the Iberian and the colonial elites. England, on the other hand, had developed its own merchant marine with state support, which allowed the establishment of trading depots in Africa, Asia, and the Western Hemisphere. The British acquisition of Caribbean islands enabled England to export slaves and industrial products, as well as to produce sugar and dyes and to deal in precious metals. England traded legally through intermediaries in Seville, and by piracy and smuggling in the Caribbean. From the middle of the seventeenth century, England, with the implicit collaboration of the Iberian elites, forced Spain and Portugal to lower the custom duties on British manufactured products. Thus, the Iberian oligopolists became major intermediaries and retailers. To some extent, the Western European nations imitated the English example in their commercial relations with Iberia and its colonies. The so-called triangular exchange, composed of European manufactured products, African slaves, and precious metals, sugar, tobacco, and dyes from Latin America had the Caribbean as one of its most important angles. Unlike in the English development of its productive forces, Iberia had not promoted the growth of a commercial bourgeoisie. Moreover, Iberia experienced a profound economic decay. All the dynastic projects for the political unity of Iberia were stopped in 1640 when Portugal revolted against Spanish rule.

Commerce between Spain and its colonies was jointly administered by the House of Trade and the Consulado (the guild of merchants) located in Seville until 1700, when it was moved to Cadiz. During most of the colonial period the House of Trade and Consulado maintained their monopolies and privileges. The House of Trade was a state institution, but its members had very close relations with the Consulado, involving family, marriage, and ethnic networks. In order to control trade, bureaucratic appointments, emigration and immigration to and from the colonies, and to set the dates when the Spanish fleets left for the colonies and returned, both institutions collaborated in an intertwining relationship. The Consulado collected the *avería* (fee for military protection) from merchant vessels that traded with colonies. Until the Bourbon Reforms of the eighteenth century, the Spanish trade was officially channeled through three American ports: Cartagena, Portobelo, and Veracruz. Legal exchanges of limited European products for abundant precious metals and Spanish American coins took place in those ports. Legally or otherwise, English and Western European merchants from the outset participated in alliances with local intermediaries and monopolists in the colonial trade. Indianos (both Spaniards and criollos), after having accumulated wealth in the colonies, returned to Spain and also participated in those entrepreneurial transactions. They were mixed family clans who owned enterprises on both sides of the Atlantic. The extended family links among the merchant elite, the Andalucian landowners, and the royal bureaucrats were closely intertwined. They were monopolist forces with aristocratic aspirations, opposed to the modernization of the Spanish mercantilist system. These elites, first in Seville and afterward in Cadiz, were afraid to lose their monopolies.

They defended their privileges by even opposing the creation of anonymous share-holding companies. Just as the refeudalization of contemporary Eastern Europe was intertwined with the industrialization of Western Europe, Iberia and its colonies followed an analogous path.

The development of maritime technology enabled Portugal to have a virtual monopoly in the trade of spices, silks, and porcelains in the Indian Ocean during the sixteenth century. The Portuguese discovery of Brazil in 1500 was of secondary importance in Portugal's colonial strategy. Thus, it established only small enclaves for the collection of *pau do brasil* (red wood dyes) on the Brazilian coast. The Portuguese and other European adventurers who explored the South American Atlantic coast in search of gold discovered the River Plate (River of Silver). According to the cronistas, Peru (Virú) and the River Plate were discovered almost at the same time (1516). It has been assumed that the silver traded by the Europeans originated in the Inca Empire, but Mojo Indians of southern Bolivia had been exchanging precious metals from the Andes for tropical products from the River Plate basin from the remotest pre-Inca times. The existence of Andean silver further increased the utopian fantasies of European adventurers and the explorations on both coasts of South America. The French were already organizing alliances with the Tomoi and Carijo Indians against the Portuguese. The danger of French enclaves in Brazilian territory forced the Portuguese crown to promote a more extensive colonization. Such efforts resulted in the rise of large sugar plantations between Recife and Salvador during the second half of the sixteenth century. However, the French and their Indian allies continued to be a threat to the Portuguese colonization until the second decade of the seventeenth century.

After the Portuguese discovery of Brazil, only small enclaves emerged where European trinkets were bartered for dye wood. The encounter between Europeans and the native Tupi speakers was one of friendly trade. The Portuguese married important Indian women in local ceremonies; their children, the Mestizos or Mamelucos, would help defeat the Indians who struggled to expel the Whites from Brazil. When Portuguese gangs, together with Mamelucos and their

Indian families, were almost defeated by the Tupinamba Indians and their French allies, the Portuguese crown took direct control of the colonization process. But the intensification of the colonization also brought the enslavement of the natives. The Portuguese brutality against the defeated Indians was as intense as that of the Spanish conquerors, and it was in the Brazilian Amazon where Indian slavery lasted the longest in the Americas. The Mamelucos would figure as the most infamous hunters of "enemy Indians" or *negros da terra* (local Blacks). The conquest of Brazil was intimately related to the Mamelucos. The first Mamelucos produced the *bandeiras* and *bandeirantes*, who constituted the vanguard of the Brazilian colonization and Indian-hunting.[100] However, in the enclave and plantation economy, African slaves became the dominant labor force from 1580 to the end of the colonial period.

Although Indians and Africans continued revolting and escaping to the tropical jungle during the entire colonial period, the African survivors were the most notable and numerous. In the distant uncolonized regions emerged *quilombos*, where fugitive slaves found sanctuary. The *quilombos*, like the Spanish American *palenques*, became the most famous refugee centers for runaway slaves. Perhaps the most famous quilombo was the so-called Palmares Republic (Alagôas), in which ten Afro-Brazilian towns resisted Portuguese and Dutch control for almost the whole seventeenth century. Recent research confirms Indian collaboration and especially women's assistance in the Palmares resistance.[101] The runaway slaves were not defeated by the Portuguese crown and the bandeirantes until 1694. A year later, Ganga Zimba, the leader of the Palmares resistance, was murdered and beheaded. However, Indians continued attacking White settlements even after Brazil became independent. Until the middle of the nineteenth century, some parts of the Brazilian coast were totally uninhabitable for Whites because of Indian attacks.

The Jesuits supported the Portuguese crown religiously and even militarily in the subjugation of the Brazilian Indians. After the Indians were defeated, the Jesuits became the most important custodians of their freedom and labor. The Indians were congregated in *aldeias*, adjacent to Portuguese cities, and later on in distant missions. The aldeias were a source of labor and income for the crown and the church in exchange for Indian Christianization. In some ways, the aldeias functioned like the Indian reductions and congregations in Spanish America, in that landowners and entrepreneurs could requisition paid Indian workers from the aldeias. However, only a small percentage of Indians lived in the aldeias, since the majority were hunted in what were termed "just wars." The aldeias were managed by Catholic orders, particularly the Jesuits, until 1757, after which the aldeias were put under civilian and military jurisdiction.

In Brazil, the Catholic Church did not achieve the opulence of its Spanish American counterpart, but until the Jesuit expulsion (1759), this order was the largest landowner. It was also the most powerful religious order. The Jesuits were the most tenacious users of African slaves and Indian servants in Iberian America. Steadfastly opposed by the settlers, the Jesuits were constantly accused of challenging the Portuguese crown and interfering in the relations between the king and his Indian vassals. In Portuguese America, priests and friars profited in entrepreneurial ventures of almost every type. They traded for the benefit of their religious institutions and their own private interests. It is not without reason that they were prohibited from entering Minas Gerães for being gold smugglers in 1711.

When the Brazilian Indians refused to be enslaved, and fled to the immense Amazon jungle, landowners imported African slaves. With the subsequent expansion in sugarcane and tobacco cultivation, the demand for African slaves increased. The enclave plantation was invented in Brazil. About two and a half million Africans were brought to work as slaves during the colonial period. However, the profits from the entrepreneurial ventures in Asia, Africa, and Brazil were not invested in the modernization or industrialization of Portugal. The success of Portuguese monarchical capitalism survived until the second decade of the seventeenth century; at its zenith, the Portuguese king was considered the richest of Europe.[102] In the first half of the seventeenth century, the Dutch forced the Portuguese to diminish their presence in Asia, and between 1630 and 1654, they captured the sugar-producing area of northeastern Brazil. Moreover, the Dutch and the British began to produce sugar for export in the Caribbean. Little by little, the British embraced a more aggressive policy and seized commercial and hegemonic spaces from the Dutch. But despite British expansionism, Holland survived as the European banker until the end of the eighteenth century.

By the end of the sixteenth century, Spanish mercantilism had developed mining centers in Mexico and Peru as well as agricultural and cattle-raising zones that supplied the mining and urban centers. The main purpose of mining and colonial entrepreneurship was to supply the Spanish metropolis with precious metals. It was mostly through the Indian tribute and labor that the colonizers had built a mercantile, extractive, and mining economy. The colonial enterprises were dynamic and were deeply affected by international supply and demand. The internal relations of production were not static; for example, in the mining industry, workers ranged from the best international mineralogists to slaves and semislaves of all races. Among the wage earners there were Whites, Mestizos, and Indians, but the majority of workers were neither White nor free. As a result of all this activity, the city of Potosí, a booming mining town, suddenly surpassed London's population during the seventeenth century.

The efforts of Columbus and the Portuguese to export Amerindian slaves for the European market failed. Instead the Latin American colonies would become labor importers, and most workers were not wage earners. Wherever natives were scarce, Africans were imported to work in bondage. Spain, which controlled more Amerindians than all the other European colonizing powers combined, imported about a million African slaves during the colonial period. More Blacks than Whites migrated to Brazil and Spanish America during the colonial period. But Amerindian bondage in Spanish America was first implanted through the *encomienda* and *repartimiento*. The Latin American colonies developed a mixed labor system with the coexistence and interrelation of wage earners and several forms of slavery and semislavery. However, the most characteristic type of work was coercive. Even the wage-earning workers were not entirely free.

The encomienda in Spanish America, and the first captaincies granted to twelve Portuguese *donatarios*, involved concessions of authority to colonizers and private entrepreneurs in exchange for specific contributions to the imperial projects of the crown. The Spanish and Portuguese monarchs, like those of other European countries, were not prepared to use their own funds to start and finance colonialist development outside Europe. In various forms, private enterprise pioneered the development of colonial regimes. Subsequently, all the European governments would make great efforts to recover the authority delegated to their entrepreneurs and private agents. Along with the European colonial expansion emerged centralized states under the sponsorship of monarchical authorities. In Spain and Portugal, the *letrados* (college graduates) led the bureaucratization process, becoming more of a professional elite than a social class.[103] A kind of hereditary meritocracy soon expanded in the bureaucracy of the Iberian world.

The Spanish kings, like the Portuguese monarchs, had their elitist councils (*consejos, conselhos*) and favorites who helped them rule, legislate, collect taxes, and administer justice in their empires. As in other types of imperialism, the state combined legality with violence in order to prevail. At the outset, the administration of Brazil constituted only a very small part of Portuguese colonialism. With the advent of enlightened despotism during the eighteenth century, the Council of Indies (Spain) and the Overseas Council (Portugal) were reorganized and formalized into ministries. It was a quest for the professionalization and the centralization of the state apparatus in the colonies. Enlightened despotism also tried to increase state revenues in the colonies. In some ways, the intention was to take away privileges from the church, the local elites, and the caciques as well as to make tributary subjects out of the mixed races (castes). Those were capitalistic policies promoted by the state.

The first *encomenderos* (owners of encomiendas) were allowed by the Spanish crown to obtain tribute in products and labor from the Indians in exchange for their Christianization. In the beginning, the encomienda was often referred to as "repartimiento." It was an exploitation directly controlled by the encomenderos that later would pass to the supervision of the crown's *corregidores* (royal representatives). The Spanish concentrated themselves in the areas where large and diverse Amerindian populations would do the pro-

ductive work. Such a situation enabled them to make greater and
more intimate contacts with Amerindians than any other European
power in the New World. The encomienda and the repartimiento in
the frontier regions or the colonial periphery did not have the same
importance as in the Andean or Mesoamerican regions. However, in
the territorial peripheries of European colonialism in the Americas,
the relations between Whites and Indians were strikingly similar.

In the regions and centers that were already colonized by Spanish,
the repartimiento was the most important labor institution after the
middle of the sixteenth century. It was first institution established in
the Caribbean and was intimately connected with the encomienda.
When in 1542 the crown prohibited the encomenderos from procuring free Indian labor, the econcomienda and the repartimiento
became legally distinct. In the future, the Indians would have to pay
their tribute to the state in money or products. The colonial state
would emerge as the legal moderator in the exploitation of Indians
while promoting the market economy among them. By the end of the
sixteenth century, the colonial state had established a centralized
apparatus for exploiting labor from the ethnic communities. Government bureaucracy began to monopolize the tribute collection and
the assigning of Indian workers to private enterprises.

Labor assignment took place under various regional names such as
the *mita* (Peru) and *cuatequil* (Mexico). The great difference between the cuatequil and the mita was that in the first case, the workers lived near their workplaces, while the *mitayos* traveled long distances and worked for longer periods. In those days, miners or White
entrepreneurs obtained mitayos through a request to the colonial
authorities that a number of workers be assigned for some tasks to
perform certain periods. The mitayos were assigned to the applicants
according to the number of inhabitants in the ethnic communities.
The applicant promised to pay the mitayo the salary determined by
the assigning authorities. In many cases the right to apply for mitayos
had a hereditary character.[104] The White applicants could also sub-
lease their mitayos.[105] The mitayos were paid an insufficient salary for
survival. In order to survive, they brought their own food and supplies from their home regions. In addition, some ethnic communities

were able to develop a supply system for their recruited mitayos. The links between the ethnic community and the serving mitayos were never completely broken. Mitayos who survived this semislavery were allowed to return to their own ethnic communities. In the Andean mining centers, even the wage-earning Indians maintained reciprocity contacts and obligations with their own ethnic communities.[106]

After Potosí was discovered (1545) and until 1601, almost fifty percent of the world's silver came from its veins.[107] More than a million mitayos would perish in Potosí between 1545 and 1745. All Indian adult males from the Peruvian Andes were subject to the Potosí mita for one year out of seven. The Count De Lemos and Peruvian viceroy noted in 1670: "The stones and minerals of Potosí are bathed in Indian blood and if one is to squeeze the extracted money, more blood than silver will gush out."[108] The colonial economy and especially the mining industry promoted an internal market for textiles and artisan goods produced in *obrajes* (sweatshops); Indians who worked there met with the nearly the same tragic fate as those who worked in the mines. Only in Peru were children and elderly Indians forced by the colonial authorities to work in the obrajes.[109] Indian-hunters were sent out to capture fugitives from the repartimiento and obrajes. These bounty hunters were mostly Mestizos and outlaws; in the Andes they were called *guatacos*.[110]

The obrajes had an Iberian origin and were first started in Mexico during the early 1530s. To supply the demand for textiles, obrajes were established throughout the colonies with state support. Unlike the European obrajes, where the municipal guilds and professional masters were the organizers, in the colonies, econcomenderos, corregidores, priests, and friars became the entrepreneurs. The obrajes became the first industrial organizations of the Americas. The larger obrajes had between four and five hundred permanent workers. In the beginning, Spanish American textiles were almost as good as those from Spain, but state limitations imposed in order to protect the supposedly finer Spanish products retarded the local textile industry. The boom for Spanish American textiles lasted until the end of the seventeenth century. With the accession of the Bourbons,

greater restrictions were imposed on the Peruvian and Mexican obrajes. The elimination of customs restrictions for English and European
textiles also accelerated the decline of the local industries. However,
fine vicuña woolens continued to be illegally exported.

Work in the obrajes was constant and terribly feared by the Indians. The Peruvian historian Fernando Silva Santisteban perceptively notes: "When the Indians were informed by the cacique or governor which of them must make up the mita for the obrajes, the most
extreme anguish overcame them . . . many preferred to escape to the
most distant and unknown regions and would seek to die by what-
ever means."[111] Even the Jesuits who supposedly protected their Indians forced them to produce piecework in their obrajes. When the
mitayos did not fulfill their quotas, harsh physical punishments were
inflicted upon them.[113] The Catholic orders kept their own jails for
the Indian shamans and priestesses, who were also forced to work in
the obrajes. Extirpators of idolatries, among whom the Jesuits were
notorious, condemned Indian witches to the slow death of the
obrajes.[113]

The Spanish crown considered the repartimiento to be a temporal
institution that eventually had to be abolished. Therefore, by the end
of the sixteenth century, the crown began to impose restrictions on
the repartimiento outside the mining industry, and it encouraged the
importation of African slaves. For example, the repartimientos in the
sugar mills were prohibited. However, forced labor went on despite
the laws and any good intentions. Bribery and complicity between
the applicants for mitayos and the local authorities continued, and
the hunting of Indians did not stop. In the final analysis, the condition
of the Indian masses as slaves, semislaves, or nominally free people
made very little difference in their daily survival. Under colonial domination, the Indians were tormented, worked hard, were malnour-
ished, and suffered epidemics. The social, moral, and spiritual character of pre-Columbian work was transformed into European physical
and economic categories.[114] Two Spanish scientists, naturalists who
visited and studied South America during the eighteenth century, recommended: "The master must have his eye continually upon them
[Indians]: for whenever he turns his back, the Indian immediately

leaves off working."[115] The participatory enjoyment of human labor disappeared, and reciprocity between the rulers and the ruled was terminated. In various forms and ways, some Indian ethnic communities were able to finance the exclusion of their members from the mita. The *faltriquera* (pocket) Indians substituted for the mitayos for a fee. These pocket Indians were paid, and they were allowed to work for their own benefit in the mines during Sundays and holidays. Such a practice left the royal treasury without income, while the White entrepreneurs and miners continued to profit.

White resistance to the royal restrictions upon the repartimiento did not reach the same level of belligerence that the abolition of the encomienda created in 1542. The great difference was that unlike before, there was no longer a social class that depended on the encomienda for its survival and development. Debt peonage had emerged. This institution had its origins in the late sixteenth century, but it rapidly expanded during the following two centuries, and it persisted even after Latin American independence. This system of labor indebtedness consisted of small loans made by the landowners to the Indians, who could then pay tithes, tributes, and other obligations in exchange for their labor. Labor indebtedness could be inherited by the children and relatives of the Indian victims from generation to generation. Moreover, throughout the Latin American colonial world, powerful landowners and miners were able to control labor wages and keep them low.

Epidemics of European diseases, malnutrition, and forced labor caused the Indian demographic catastrophe in the times of the Iberian conquest. The Caribbean Indians were virtually annihilated in half a century of Spanish occupation. There were twenty-five million inhabitants before the conquest of Mexico, but a century later there were only about a million; from almost thirty million people in the Inca Empire, the population decreased to less than a million in 1754. The Indian demographic recovery in Mesoamerica began in the middle of the seventeenth century, while in the Andes the population began increasing in the eighteenth century.[116] The pre-Columbian Brazilian population has been calculated at between one and two and a half million.[117] The demographic catastrophe of Brazilian Indians was almost permanent. The great Amerindian depopulation was the main cause of the decay of the Mexican and Peruvian mining industry that began by the late sixteenth century, and it created the opportunity for the development of the large landed estates of Latin America. With the decline of the mining boom during the seventeenth century, the great Mexican haciendas subtly were converted into semi-isolated and almost self-sufficient estates with feudalistic characteristics,[118] while in Peru a more entrepreneurial diversification emerged.[119] The deterioration of trade between Europe and Iberian America promoted the development of local industries and the regionalization of markets in the colonies.[120] With the decline of the export economy, it was even tolerated that some Indians might escape from the congregations and reductions.[121] While Iberia really converted itself into a semiperiphery of the British metropolis, Iberian American institutions, population, and society developed a local flavor and stabilized themselves.

During the seventeenth century, the criollo elites acquired hegemony within the colonial state. The crown's authority weakened, while the criollos utilized the bureaucracy to increase their fortunes. Indeed, the century of Spanish decadence led to times of plenty and baroque refinements for the colonies. The European economic expansion and the intensification of colonization in the American continent caused new demographic pressures and dislocations during the eighteenth century. Tensions intensified, not only between Whites and Indians, but also between Spaniards and criollos. The Indian rebellions were intimately interrelated with their old political and legal resistance against Spanish colonialism. Local protests and routine mobilizations were transformed into struggles that tried to eliminate the European domination, and in some cases, race wars developed. From the margins of the Amazon Basin to the American Midwest, frontier conflicts between Europeans and Indians intensified, giving rise to such revolutionary figures as Juan Santos Atahualpa (1742–1752) and Pontiac (1763). However, only in the nuclear centers of European colonization, in the movement of Tupac Amaru II (1780–81), for example, would the revolts become real anticolonialist revolutions. Although it has been noted that the Tupac Amaru movement had

internal ethnic problems, those were not the major reasons for its failure. Tupac Amaru II relied on a plan for multiethnic and class collaboration that was defeated.[122] Even though there were conflicts
between local ethnic groups and *forasteros* (newly resettled Indians),
the defeat of this Andean utopia was more the result of the fragmentation in rural interests.[123]

When ethnic communities adjacent to the Spanish American landed estates were forced to pay tribute in products and work to the
colonial state, they became persuaded and pressured through small
loans by the White landowners to live within their haciendas. Thus,
the basis for the debt peonage system was born. Gradually the hacienda became a sanctuary for the Indians where the landowner provided paternalistic protection in exchange for work and obedience. The
hacienda owners were lords with self-appointed civil and criminal
jurisdiction within their estates. Paradoxically, Indian subordination
became violent and stable simultaneously.

The Indians were intimidated to be submissive and respectful of
the Whites and their interests. With the arrival of the eighteenth century, the haciendas began to produce on a large scale as the result of
the growing regional and international demand for agricultural and
pastoral products for the export market. This was especially the case
in the Spanish American periphery, such as Cuba, Venezuela, and the
River Plate region. However, this export process had already been
started in Brazil and the Caribbean during the sixteenth century, with
their sugar plantations. The sugar industry was first developed in
Hispaniola, but the crown promoted its deterioration because it com-
peted with sugar production in the Canary Islands. With the decline
of the Brazilian sugar industry in the beginning of the eighteenth century, the Caribbean sugar plantations owned by the British, Dutch,
and French took over entrepreneurial leadership.[124] Precious metals
and sugar were the major export products during the long colonial
period of Latin America.

Colonial Latin American society was pigmentocratic from its outset, and despite so-called progress and democratic rhetoric, a racist
heritage persists until today. "The whiter the better" is still an applic-
able proverb. It was an axiom that color and phenotype determined

wealth, power, and social position. At the beginning of the Spanish conquest, the racial mixture between the conquistadores and women of the local nobility was supported by the crown because those unions promoted collaboration in the colonialist project. Such a policy gave more opportunities to Indian women than to Indian men for scaling the social ladder of the colonial patriarchal system.[125] As wives, mistresses, servants, and prostitutes, Amerindian women were intimately involved in the daily lives of the conquerors, but, as more White men and women arrived, Amerindian women and Mestizos were pushed aside from the power structure, and "many Spaniards preferred to marry a white prostitute [rather] than an Indian woman."[126]

Many Mestizos were considered better harquebusiers than the Spaniards, and the fear developed that they could become leaders, competing with Whites. The importation of African slaves added a new color shade to the racial mixture and pigmentocracy. The colonial jurists tried to develop a "republic" of Spaniards and another of Indians but despite the crown's efforts to promote racial separation instead of integration, castes or mixed-bloods emerged, and eventually became the most rapidly expanding group. However, the colonial fears that Mestizos, Mulattos, and castes would lead Indian or Afro-American revolts motivated the crown, beginning in the sixteenth century, to sanction the legal isolation of colored people. In 1554, the viceroy of New Spain, Luis de Velasco, asserted that the Mestizos "are growing in great numbers and all of them are so badly inclined and so audacious for all the wickedness that one has to fear them and the Blacks . . . and the Indians get from them so many bad manners."[41]

With the passing of time, the Spanish considered even the criollos, children of Europeans born in the New World, to be inferior. The fact that some of them had a small percentage of Indian blood in their veins evoked contempt from the Spanish. However, for more than three centuries Spaniards and criollos lived together and constituted an allied elite that facilitated the longevity of the colonial system. In addition, since at the outset not many White women came, casual miscegenation by right of conquest rapidly expanded. The Mestizos and castes became subordinate allies and intermediaries in the oppression and exploitation of Indians. Despite the fact that Mestizos and castes had the stigma of being illegitimate children, their racial mixture facilitated their exemption from the Indian tribute and other servile obligations. They aspired to become Whites, and when possible, they searched for marital partners of lighter skin. Even with obstacles and restrictions small groups of castes advanced in the social ladder. But when the castes came to the top, they had to behave like Whites and defend the bias and interests of the system. This is the prototype of social mobility that has survived until today.

Generally, Mestizos and castes moved to the urban centers, where they could become artisans. The urban centers became the main centers for the mixed populations. Moreover, the social convulsions caused by the Spanish conquest increased the dislocation of the forastero Indians (outsider natives), who already lived away from their ethnic communities in pre-Columbian times. They were Indians who did not have a specific occupation. Some of the forastero Indians possessed their own lands. In the Spanish cities, if they took White partners, they could become Mestizos. Since in the cities the Indians could learn Spanish occupations, they could earn enough money to hire their substitutes for the repartimiento. In the cities, the Spanish guilds allowed the castes and even Indians to become apprentices, but only the Whites could be professional masters. In some cases, even the apprentices had to be White, as was the situation of the Mexican goldsmiths during the eighteenth century. When the castes were allowed to enroll in the colonial militia in the eighteenth century, a new possibility for social climbing was opened, especially for those with lighter skins. The castes, Indians, and Blacks who served in the colonial militia were placed in special units under the command of White officers. The independence movement led by criollos created one more chance for the colored peoples who aspired to become what would be the Latin Americans of the future.

In the areas of the so-called high Amerindian cultures, the conquistadores married the daughters of the *indios principales* (Indian nobility). Many of them returned with their children to Spain and were granted appointments and interviews with the Spanish monarchs. Some built castles and entered the Spanish military orders. The

Mestizo descendants of Montezuma and the Incas were granted nobility by the crown. A Mestizo woman, a descendant of Montezuma, married the viceroy of New Spain. In 1701, this viceroy was granted the title Count of Montezuma. The niece of Tupac Amaru I married the nephew of Ignatius of Loyola; their heirs were granted the title Marquis of Oropesa. The sister of Atahualpa had a daughter by Francisco Pizarro; she married her uncle, Hernando Pizarro. Marriages of this sort strengthened the claim of properties and nobility titles in the colonies and Spain. Especially in Mexico and the Andes, a Mestizo aristocracy emerged at the dawn of the Spanish conquest. The fact that the count of Montezuma became the viceroy of New Spain did not mean, of course, that the Aztecs had regained power. Many Latin American criollos today trace their genealogy to Indian princesses and conquistadores.

The caciques who collaborated with the Spanish conquest held the title Natural Lord, the same title held by the Spanish monarchs. Those caciques petitioned the Spanish monarchs for special favors. Many of them were granted coats of arms and were elevated to the rank of Natural Conquerors. The cacique negotiated with the colonial bureaucracy for the interests of his ethnic community as well as for his own traditional privileges. Despite the cultural limitations of the reciprocity principle between caciques and ethnic communities, exploitation in the relations of production was intensified during the colonial period, and even afterward. As a general rule, the caciques collaborated in the White exploitation and oppression of the ethnic communities. The fact that there were not enough Whites to administer the colonial system at all levels gave the Indian nobility the opportunity of becoming intermediaries in the relations between the Whites and the Indian masses. It is because of this that the destruction of the Amerindian governments among the high cultures was a selective process during the Spanish conquest. The Indian nobility was exempted from the tribute, the repartimiento, and other servile obligations. At the outset of the colonial period, their children were educated at special schools for nobles. Indian women and men who did not marry White partners could buy certificates that accredited their whiteness. White accreditation brought some privileges similar

Colonial ethnicity according to Guaman Poma (seventeenth century, Peru).

to those of the real Whites, such as owning horses and African slaves. At the beginning of the seventeenth century, Guaman Poma would accuse those Indian racial climbers of "moral decadence."[42]

In order to socially discipline and rationalize production in the Spanish mode, the ethnic communities were Christianized, urbanized, and reduced. The reductions were especially harmful in the Andean region, where the pre-Columbian agricultural production had been organized by the Inca state according to the ecological zones.

Colonial obrajes under the control of Catholic orders (seventeenth century, Peru).

The Andean communities, through social reciprocities, redistributed goods and supported themselves with products from various ecologies. Only in this manner had the Incas avoided the regional famines of many pre-Columbian Amerindians and other peoples of the world. In the end, Andean peoples under the hegemony of Western civilization would experience the ravages of famine.

The ethnic communities that had collaborated in the Spanish conquest were organized as *cacicazgos* (cacique fiefdoms) by their leaders. For the caciques, hispanization was a system of authority and a way to maintain authority. In some cases the cacicazgos were inherited from generation to generation according to the Spanish system of primogeniture. All the large ethnic communities were gradually organized according to Spanish laws. In such cases, the Indian nobility controlled the municipal councils, mayors, and magistrates. The Indian elites became the real collectors of the Indian tribute for the crown. By the eighteenth century, small groups of extremely rich and aristocratic caciques had emerged, who owned great cacicazgos as well as much cattle, Black slaves, sugar mills, real estate, and ships. Some caciques had become the major producers of European wines in the Peruvian Viceroyalty.[43] The traveler and scientist Alexander von Humboldt, who visited Lima at the beginning of the nineteenth century, informs us about Don Dionisio Yupanqui, a very wealthy direct descendant of the Incas, whom everybody respected and greeted. The same can be said of the cacique of Cajamarca, Patricio Astopilco, by the end of the colonial period. Both were actually Mestizos and had White relatives. Dionisio Yupanqui became the Peruvian representative at the Spanish Cortes that fought against Napoleon's invasion of Iberia. However, the caciques as a social class had lost importance. By then, the success of the caciques basically depended on their entrepreneurial capacities, just like the White landowners. Indeed, they had already been assimilated into the "republic" (society) of Spaniards.

Unlike the Andean criollos of the eighteenth century, the Mexican criollos had already assimilated several Aztec symbols and traditions as their own.[130] Even though the Indian revolts of Mexico intensified during the eighteenth century, they would be definitively contained by the republic of the Spaniards.[131] In Peru as well as Mexico, many caciques and the Indian nobles supported the republic of the Spaniards, but Andean messianism and utopias constituted a greater ideological challenge to the Hispanic-Peruvian protonationalism. Indeed, in the southern Andes, "the caciques of the post-conquest" and an Indian nobility emerged to challenge the power of the Lima merchant aristocracy.[132] Furthermore, because of the European expansionism of the eighteenth century, Indian prophets and Amerindian protonationalists emerged, from those in the Andes to the Algonquins of Canada. This ethnoreligious messianism is analogous to the first native movements against European colonialism in Africa, Asia, and the South Pacific.

In the Peruvian viceroyalty there were fewer Whites and Mestizos than in Mexico by the end of the colonial period. In Peru the republics of Spaniards and Indians were more clearly visible. Moreover, a cultural Incan renaissance had emerged that attracted even some Mestizos and criollos during the eighteenth century. Andean messianism predicted the return of a native savior called Inkarri who would bring a new era of happiness. *The Royal Commentaries* written by the Mestizo Garcilaso Inca de la Vega (1539–1616), which discusses good government, justice, and material abundance during Incan rule, became a subversive document and generator of utopias. The Indian militancy intensified. It has been recorded that between 1720 and 1790, more than one hundred revolts took place against the colonial authorities in Peru and Upper Peru (Bolivia). Moreover, in an area inhabited by 1,200,000 people, about 100,000 persons died in the Andean revolts of Tupac Amaru II and Tupac Katari (1780–82). Despite the internal divisions of several kinds, these revolts contained a proto-Amerindian nationalism that involved collaboration among distinct ethnic groups. The ethnic collaboration between Quechuas and Aymaras was concluded by the marriage between the nephew of Tupac Amaru II and Tupac Katari's sister.

The mobilization of the entire military colonial apparatus as well as the use of mostly Black soldiers[133] defeated the biggest Amerindian independence movement in the Western Hemisphere. As on previous occasions, the Indian movement toward liberation was suppressed with the help of pro-Spanish caciques.[134] The most important cacique in the repression of the Tupac Amaru movement was Mateo Pumacahua (1748–1815), a direct descendent of Emperor Huayna Capac. The Pumacahua clan distinguished itself for its services to the crown and the loyalty of its Indian masses. Ironically, when Pumacahua participated in the criollo independence movement, he was captured by the Indians and handed over to the Spaniards, who executed him.[135] Despite the fact that the ethnic group Maranganí captured Pumacahua, by this time Indian self-identification among the native Amerindians was much more socially and ethnically inclusive than at the time of the Spanish conquest.

Unlike the Mexican Indian revolts, in which criollos and castes emerged as leaders, the Andean Indians themselves led their mobilizations. As it has been well documented by the late Peruvian historian Alberto Flores Galindo, the understanding and dialogue between the republics of Indians and Spaniards was interrupted by the social conflicts and repression that erupted between 1780 and 1824.[136] Indians were prohibited from even baptizing their children with the name Inca. The pilgrims to pre-Columbian sacred places, which the

Catholic Church unwillingly tolerated, were persecuted or reoriented. For example, the Andean mountain Qoyllur Riti (Snowy Star), where the Indians venerated their ancestors, was converted into a Christian cult site. By coincidence or miracle, the Indian herdsman Mariano met the Child Jesus in 1783. Afterward, the annual pilgrimage to the Lord of Qoyllur Riti began to take place at the same time as Corpus Christi. This is still a native cult with a light Catholic disguise. In another instance, in the same decade as the Tupac Amaru revolution, the Catholic Church confirmed the miraculous appearances of the Lord of Pampamarka and the Lord of Tungasuca.[137] These miraculous appearances occurred in regions directly affected by the Tupac Amaru movement. In practical terms, they meant that priests and friars took religious and political control of the Huacas and sacred mountains.

The republic of criollos led the independence project. After the Indian rebellions of the eighteenth century and the Bourbon Reforms, the Indian elites lost most of their privileges. Even the Indian nobles who collaborated with the crown were abandoned when they were no longer needed to administer the low levels of the bureaucracy. During the Indian rebellions, the old resentments erupted in excesses against both Spaniards and criollos. The Indian chronicler Guaman Poma had already noted in the early seventeenth century that the criollos were "arrogant, lazy, liars, gamblers, swindlers and enemies of the poor Indians and of the Spaniards . . . they are worse than the Mestizos, Mulattos and Blacks."[138] Although the Indian rebellions had only temporary triumphs, the White fear of the Indians increased. The economic, political, and cultural repression of the republic of Indians intensified with ferocity. With the passing of time, the intermediary function of the Indian nobility between Whites and ethnic communities became analogous to the role of Mestizos and castes in relation to Indians and Blacks. With the growth of miscegenation, the intermediary role of the Indian nobility became less necessary.

Just as some ethnic groups enjoyed some privileges under Spanish colonialism, the less privileged classes of pre-Columbian societies had, in some cases, the opportunity to escape from the worst oppres-

sion and exploitation. For example, the semislave mayeque class of
the Aztec society continued being subordinated to the Indian upper
classes, and until the end of the sixteenth century it avoided the
cuatequil or repartimiento. Likewise, the Incan semislaves or yanaconas avoided the mita or repartimiento until the eighteenth century. In Mexico as in Peru, free Indians passed as pre-Columbian semislaves in order to avoid the repartimiento. The yanaconas of the Inca
Empire, whether temporary or permanent, generally came from the
defeated ethnic groups. With the Spanish conquest, the function of
the yanaconas drastically changed. The Spaniards classified as yanaconas all the Indians that were not in the encomiendas or reductions.
The yanaconas and their families rapidly followed the Spaniards as
their personal servants. The yanacona system was expanded by the
Whites to include nonagricultural tasks such as serving as "assistants"
(servants) in conquering wars. The yanaconas rendered personal service by turns and became sharecroppers on their new masters' lands.
They could be sold, bought, and inherited. They paid a special tribute
to the state according to the type of their occupation. By the middle
of the seventeenth century, the yanacona institution developed
regional features. Simultaneously, in the haciendas salary earners,
slaves, and yanaconas emerged. By the end of the colonial period,
there were Indians, Mestizos, castes, and even criollos among the
yanaconas of the Peruvian coast.[139]

The reappearance and transformation of the mayeques and yanaconas during the Spanish colonial era represented Indian strategies to
resist the repartimiento. The Indians struggled legally and illegally as
well as peacefully and violently. This process has been called by some
"adaptive resistance."[140] By the end of the colonial period, the wage-
earning system in Mexico was greater than in Peru. While the Mexican mining industry was controlled by a few big companies, in the
Andean region, the small mining entrepreneurs predominated. The
Mexican mining industry was led by seventeen multimillionaire families, both Indianos and criollos.[141] The repartimiento and the yanacona system were the dominant mode of production in the central
Andes, even though in some mining centers of Lower Peru the wage
earners predominated.[142] In the mining centers, the yanaconas were

paid higher salaries than the mitayos and were given the least dangerous tasks. However, the labor force was scarce in both viceroyalties.[143] The repartimiento was not eliminated in Mexico, and it continued to function as a subsidy to the mining industry until the nineteenth century.

The conquistadores were the law and power at the outset, but gradually the crown took control of colonial administration, until 1570, when the colonial bureaucracy took direct authority over the colonies. The change was the result of an interrelation of state and private interests designed to exploit the colonies for the benefit of the colonial state. The first generation of encomenderos and caciques allowed the crown only an indirect role, but the swift growth of mineral production in the American colonies activated the crown's efforts to establish a more direct control of its colonies. Until the 1570s, the Andean production of precious metals was done in guairas. In this mode of production, the caciques had more control over the refinement of precious metals, and they used this function to manipulate their relations with the Spaniards. But the amalgamation with a *patio* (mercury) process created an unusual growth of silver production.[144] The capture of Tupac Amaru I coincided with this technological revolution in the production of precious metals and the efforts of the crown to benefit directly from the mining boom.

In theory, the colonies were directly subordinated to the absolute power of the Spanish king. Only the representatives of the king could exercise final authority. In practice, the system was paternalist at all its levels, and Spaniards as well as criollos participated for mutual benefit. In the extensive colonial territory, distance diluted the absolutist character of the system. The bureaucrats were semiprofessionals who financed themselves through their salaries, private fees for services, and entrepreneurial activities. In order to function, the colonial bureaucracy had to negotiate and make concessions to local interests.

With the growth of the bureaucracy, the crown took the opportunity to sell positions in the colonial administration. The viceroy, in the name of the king, was in charge of balancing the local interests with those of the colonial system. His main function was executive. The viceroys were in charge of supervising fiscal matters, justice, subordinate appointments, labor regulation, and Indian well-being. In the beginning, the viceroys came from the highest Spanish classes, and the crown made efforts to find men with competence, honesty, and loyalty. A viceroy governed for about five years. He was controlled by the Audiencia (judicial court), which at the end of his administration would make a *residencia* (evaluation) of his administration. During his term of office, the viceroy could be visited by a high royal official, without previous announcement, to investigate his good or bad government (this event was the *visita*). In addition, the ecclesiastical authorities and the Consulado watched with great attention the policies of the viceroy. Until the Bourbon Reforms of the eighteenth century, the Audiencias functioned as the favorite fiefs of criollo interests.[145]

With the economic decline of the seventeenth century, the imperial controls deteriorated, as did the viceroys, who like the other bureaucrats made economic inroads and fortunes through their relatives, friends, clients, and corruption. In the seventeenth century, the sociopolitical power of the colonies reached a great apogee. In the so-called long century (1670–1770) of Portuguese and Spanish imperial decadence, private entrepreneurs greatly surpassed the state in profits.[146] For example, in the 1620s, eight or ten wealthy Peruvian Indiano families, who were established in Seville, controlled the European trade with Spanish South America.[147] At the outset of the seventeenth century, a group of Peruvian Indiano (Perulero) commercial houses traded the most exquisite international products in Lima's Merchant Street. The wealthiest Peruvian Indianos were millionaires, and they conducted international transactions in millions of pesos. On Lima's Merchant Street, there were at least sixty merchants with more than a hundred thousand pesos in capital.[148] Both European wholesalers and Dutch bankers preferred to trade with Peruvian Indianos because they dealt with gold and silver.[149] The Lima merchant aristocracy became the most important in Spanish America, and supported its expansion through commerce.[150] In addition, by the dawn of the seventeenth century, Brazilian entrepreneurs had converted Brazil into the greatest sugar producer of the world. Indeed, it was the Brazilian elite that made it possible for Portugal to maintain jurisdiction over contemporary Brazil.

The economic cycles of Iberian and Iberian American mercantilism caused the reorientation of entrepreneurial ventures in the colonies. The socioeconomic power of the criollos became hegemonic during the seventeenth century. The landowners, miners, merchants, and the church became the main financial sources of the colonial system. The *cabildos* and *senados da câmera* (municipal councils), despite their limited jurisdictions, remained in the hands of the *vecinos principales* (Iberian American elites) during the whole colonial period; they were mini-oligarchies. The creation of the viceroyalties of La Plata and New Granada by the Bourbons in the eighteenth century was, among other things, an effort of the crown to wrest power away from the Peruvian Indiano aristocracy and Iberian American entrepreneurs in South America.

It has been noted that the cross and the sword acted together in the colonial enterprise. The church defended the divinity of the Iberian monarchs, and the colonial state validated the ecumenical authority of Catholicism. Religious salvation and submission to the colonial system were the fundamental focuses of Catholic activism among Amerindians. Indians faced the dilemma of sin and rebelliousness or salvation and submission. From the outset, betrayal to the state became the equivalent of heresy. The pope granted to the Iberian crowns the royal patronage (*patronato, padroado*), which theoretically allowed the state to supervise the whole ecclesiastical apparatus. The royal patronage included the appointment, administration, and collection of funds for the Christianization of Indians and the church's sustenance. In Spanish America the religious hierarchy functioned vertically by supporting the viceroy at the top of the bureaucracy down to the corregidor at the bottom. As a general rule, the corregidores and the priests were White, and especially Spaniards. Despite all the legal limitations, the priests and corregidores engaged in entrepreneurial ventures. Both had creditors, resources, and institutions that supported and served them. It was a bureaucratic-religious system on the road to capitalist underdevelopment.

The corregidores acquired wealth with the blessings of the local priest or friar. It was a situation of mutual support at the lowest local level. The post of corregidor was obtained through payment (the wages of one year, one-half year, one month, etc.), family connections, and special favors. The wages of the corregidores were low, and often they had indebted themselves to merchants and financiers in order to obtain their positions. Although such practices permitted the crown to maintain a bureaucracy at low cost, the bureaucrats served their own interests better than those of the king. Legally, one of the obligations of the corregidor was to keep watch against the abuses and extortion by the Whites against Indians, but that was like allowing the fox to protect the chickens. The corregidores did not live from their wages, but from their entrepreneurial activities. They had an economic monopoly in their districts. The corregidor had the authority to obtain tribute and mitayos from the caciques to work in the mines, obrajes, and other enterprises. The corregidor coercively distributed European products and trinkets that the Indians did not really wish to buy. This policy was called *reparto comercial* (commercial partition). The reparto comercial emerged at the dawn of the colonial period, but it became institutionalized by the end of the seventeenth century.

The newly appointed corregidores were supported by the merchants and financiers. This relationship had the consequence of forcing the Indians to consume leftover merchandise as well as to produce export crops. The reparto comercial served to integrate the most distant Indian provinces of the colonial periphery into the regional economy according to the growing specialization and division of labor. It would become one of the most important mechanisms for obtaining labor-plus-value from the Indian workers as well as their incorporation into the regional and international market. It prevailed due to the hegemony of the state apparatus, and because there were needs for exchange and production among the Indians.[151]

The bureaucratic changes sponsored by the Bourbons were supposedly made in order to bring justice, honesty, and impartiality to administrative decisions. It was to be a rational and humanitarian administrative modernization. But the eighteenth century was a period of an arms race among the European powers. The Bourbons decided that the majority of fiscal revenues from Spain and the colonies should be used for military modernization. The interests of the military complex were mobilized at all the levels of the colonial apparatus.[152] Above all, it was a state effort to modernize itself along the lines of England and Western Europe. Motives of fairness and humanitarian impulses played a secondary role. The Bourbons sponsored a redefinition of the principles that legitimized the Spanish domination of the colonies. Beginning in the middle of the eighteenth century, Bourbon modernization had made efforts to increase the fiscal revenues: this precipitated Indian rebellions.

One of the main reasons for the rebellion of Tupac Amaru II was the increase and reorganization of the Indian tribute by the Bourbons.[153] The Bourbons imposed taxes on *chuño* (potato starch), coca leaves, grains, *charqui* (dried meat), and textiles produced by the ethnic communities and the caciques. After the Indian revolts (1780–82), the crown proclaimed the Intendant Ordinances in Peru (1784) and Mexico (1786). The Corregimientos were abolished and replaced by the Intendencias. The Intendants and Subdelegates were more professional and better paid, in order to promote good government. Spaniards and criollos, with all their clients, resisted the bureaucratic reforms. The Indians themselves, who had been indoctrinated and disciplined by almost three centuries of patriarchal rule, were baffled. In the majority of cases they were not accustomed to the use of money or its function in a free market, and they were abused by the reparto comercial as well as by the new power brokers. In Mexico and Peru, the same Intendants and Subdelegates reestablished the illicit profiteering that had already been practiced by the corregidores. In addition, landowners struggled to retain their control of the Indian labor force and sabotaged the Bourbon reforms. The old and new entrepreneurs fought for monopolies over the defenseless Indian customers. Moreover, the former monopolist merchants always insisted on maintaining their exclusive customer markets. The colonial mercantilist and extractive economy, based on neofeudal rules of labor control, entered into a new crisis that finally facilitated criollo independence from the metropolis. The Bourbon reforms of free trade hurt the interests of the Spanish American mercantile aristocracy. However, this elite kept its loyalty to the crown for fear of rebellions by Indians, Black slaves, and castes.

The priests were economically supported by the tithes and by other religious payments from the Indians. Although the Indians were legally exempted from the tithe, in practice, they were almost never really exempt. Moreover, the church auctioned the collection of the tithe to *cobradores* (collectors), another group of profiteers in search of Indian victims. The threat of eternal damnation by priests and friars was a powerful instrument for the church to persuade the old Christians as well as the neophyte Indian believers. The church administered and financed religious and public charitable institutions such as schools and hospitals. It rented urban and rural real estate as well as producing sugar, wines, textiles, and numerous other products. The Jesuits were great ranchers and exporters of sugar, cacao, flours, medicinal plants, vanilla, yerba mate tea, salted beef, and textiles. They were the wealthiest of the Catholic orders. By the end of the colonial period, the church emerged as the richest institution. Churches, convents, and monasteries with their charitable funds served as bankers, landowners, and merchants.

From the second voyage of Columbus, the Catholic orders were present in the New World. Through the royal patronage, the Vatican had granted the Iberian crowns the task of converting the recently discovered pagans. The Dominicans were the first in protesting against the abuses of the encomienda. The first conflicts between the church and the encomenderos culminated in the Laws of Burgos (1512–13). Although those laws prohibited the mistreatment of the Indians, the existence of the encomienda was confirmed. The Spanish crown also wanted to clarify its jurisdiction in the conflicts between the encomenderos and the church. The encomienda and the church had gradually become rival institutions for the physical and spiritual control of the Indians. Between the encomienda and the missions, the Indians preferred the religious fathers.

Queen Isabella is known to have prohibited Columbus from trafficking in and enslaving Indians. Those prohibitions were not absolute or without royal interest. There were exceptions and even reclamations for her percentage of the profits. King Ferdinand taxed the encomienda owners in relation to the number of their Indians, and was not very concerned about whether Indians were enslaved or not. The sale of Indian women in the Seville market was not prohibited until the middle of the sixteenth century.[154] The excuse for the imposition of Indian slavery was part of the struggle against supposed Indian cannibalism and against rebellions and resistance to European colonization. In Spanish America the innocent Indians (the collaborators) were free; that is, they could not be bought or sold; but they were subject to the encomienda. From the very beginning of White colonization in the Caribbean, Indians were subjected to the encomienda so that they could be forced to work in mining, agriculture, and ranching. Despite all prohibitions, they were bought and sold. Moreover, from the beginning of Spanish colonization, brothels that exploited mostly Indian women were opened with royal permission. Eventually Indian slavery was eliminated, but serfdom remained.

After the downfall of the pre-Columbian empires, the ethnic communities continued to retain the loyalty of their traditional members. It was on those ethnic communities that the encomenderos and the church sought to impose their jurisdiction. According to the magnanimous Father Las Casas, the Indians were rational; they constituted a special kind of non-Christians with rights to property and freedom. With the support of Charles V, Las Casas and the Dominicans successfully and peacefully Christianized the Indians from Verapaz (Guatemala) during the third decade of the sixteenth century. But, as on other occasions when the Indians were allowed to follow their consciences, they returned to their ancient spiritual beliefs and their own way of living. The religious conversions were not total, and a cosmological syncretism persists in the Indian spirituality until today.

During the third and fourth decades of the sixteenth century, a rivalry emerged between the encomendero class and the colonial state. The abolition of the encomienda by the New Laws (1542) was articulated in humanitarian terms, but the monarchical authority was also at stake. The encomenderos attempted to control the amounts and forms of the Indian tribute as well as to maintain civil and criminal jurisdiction in their regions. The crown feared the development of a feudal class like that in Europe. After the subsequent civil wars in Peru, the crown eliminated the radicalism of the New Laws. However, some restrictions against the encomienda continued. The colonial state increased its authority by taking the exclusive right to receive the Indian tribute. The tribute was the equivalent of the pecho duty paid by the Spanish lower classes. In Spanish America, Whites and those who could pass as White did not pay the tribute.

Indian tribute was maintained during the entire colonial period. Ironically, wherever the Indians were most numerous, the tribute prevailed in the independent Latin American republics until the mid-nineteenth century. Gradually, the crown ruled that encomiendas were to be valid for only one generation instead of being permanent or eternal inheritances. New efforts were made to place Indian labor under the jurisdiction and disposition of the colonial state. Royal officials began to make appraisals in order to determine how much work the encomenderos could request under the principle of "equal pay for Indians." In the monarchical offensive against the encomenderos, the church took the side of the crown. By the mid-sixteenth century, civil and religious bureaucracies agreed that henceforth conquering permits were to be granted only to "peaceful men of good conscience and defenders of God's grace." Finally, the rule that "war could not be waged against the Indians of any province in order to give them the holy Catholic faith or to make them obey us or for any other reason" was legalized in the Recopilación Laws of Indies (1680).[155]

By the end of the sixteenth century, the encomienda was a dying institution. However, the disappearance of the encomienda was primarily a consequence of the Indian demographic catastrophe. It is in this manner that the lands inhabited by Indians became *baldías* (vacant), and haciendas were built on them. The encomienda survived until the end of the colonial period, but it was no longer the main characteristic of the system. Until the end of the eighteenth century, Indians continued to pay the tribute and provide labor for the encomenderos in Paraguay, Yucatan, northwest Argentina, northern Mexico, southern Chile, and the remote areas of Central America and New Granada. The Bourbon reforms, which finally eliminated the encomienda, abolished, in reality, only a system of rents and pensions instead of a powerful socioeconomic institution. By then, the colonial aristocracy already based its wealth and authority in land, mining, and commerce instead of the previous Indian tribute and labor.

During the seventeenth century, the hacienda demand for lands began to be greater than the supply, and hacienda owners began the systematic takeover (legally or illegally) of the lands held by the surviving Indians. The Indians were requested to present property titles, and the lack of papers meant expulsion from their lands. Thus, the congregation or forced concentration of Indians in new communities emerged. The Whites ideologically defended the congregation on the supposed grounds that it would facilitate Indian religious conversion and civilization. After the Indians had been congregated in a new community, Whites strategically laid claim to the vacant Indian lands. Another way to appropriate Indian lands was by interrupting their irrigation, and when the lands had become barren, the hacienda owners bought them at reduced prices. The new owners would later restore the irrigation systems. In order to protect the Indians, the crown had stipulated from the beginning that the haciendas and the ethnic communities must be built a certain distance from each other, but in reality that would prove to be one more link in the chain of bureaucratic farces. Royal officials could disobey the crown's orders by euphemistically responding: "Obedezco pero no cumplo" (I obey but I do not comply).

The regular clergy (friars) generally dealt with the Indians, while the secular clergy (priests) ministered to the Whites. Friars and priests also disputed among each other the right to obtain labor and fees from the Indians. From the mid-sixteenth century, the Spanish crown began to side with the priests at the expense of the friars. Specifically, the friars begin to lose their parochial rights, incomes, and properties. It was the view of the crown that the missionary friars had already fulfilled their colonizing role. Only on the peripheral frontiers did the friars keep their original authority. In this manner, the missions emerged as the characteristic institution of the remote regions. Together with the presidios and military forts, the missions constituted the main instruments of the expanding Spanish frontier.

The missions took the form of towns, in which the Indians partic-

ipated in civilian and religious activities. Although the Fathers have
been credited with building the missions, it was the Indians who
were the true builders. The missions were also entrepreneurial ventures in which the Indians worked without pay in exchange for
religious charity. Thus, Indians from hunting and gathering societies
were converted into sedentary farmers. Once the nomadic Indians
were pacified, disciplined, and urbanized, the regular clergy undertook the tasks of the friars. However, the religious conversion and
labor discipline of the Indians was a very slow process in northern
Mexico, Argentina, Chile, and the Amazon region.

The Jesuit missions were unique cases, characterized by their
efficiency and prosperity. The legendary Paraguayan Jesuit missions
were built because the Brazilian bandeirantes still were hunting
Guaraní Indians, who had retreated to the Uruguay and Paraná val-
leys. On the other hand, the Spanish settlers of Paraguay pressured
the Indians from the west. In order to solve the Indian problem, the
Spanish-Portuguese crown granted the Jesuits jurisdiction over the
Indians of Ecclesiastic Paraguay in 1607. Ecclesiastic Paraguay extended from southern Bolivia to the Uruguayan northwest, including modern Paraguay, northern Argentina, parts of Mato Grosso, Paraná, Santa
Catarina, and Rio Grande do Sul. As in other parts of the Western
Hemisphere, the Jesuits created reductions, supposedly in order to
protect Indians, which included their training and equipping with
European weapons. The Jesuits and their Indians defeated the bandeirantes on the shores of the Mbororé River in 1641. Afterward, the
bandeirantes diminished their attacks on the Jesuit missions. The
Indian-Jesuit defensive capacity and the Brazilian importation of
African slaves became the main reasons for peaceful coexistence. In
1750, when the Spanish crown transferred seven Jesuit missions
to Brazil,[156] the Guarani Indians revolted on horseback and with
European arms, but they were defeated by Spanish and Portuguese
troops. The Indian defeat was a prelude to the Iberian efforts to expel
the Jesuits from their empires. Rumors about the existence of gold
mines in Jesuit territory intensified the conspiracies against them.

Discipline, music, work, and even communal property were imposed by the Jesuits upon the Indians in their missions. The "land of

God" was collectively worked, but the "land of man" was divided into individual parcels with nonnegotiable production. Tools were owned collectively. The Indians were subjected to paternalistic treatment. Food consumption was regulated, as were clothing, social behavior, working hours, resting, and worshiping times. The Indians could not make contacts outside the missions. The Jesuits of Paraguay exported mostly yerba mate tea. It has been asserted that in Paraguay, the Jesuits were inspired by the Incan social model. For example, the chasquis (relay) system was used for communication using men on horseback rather than a series of runners. In the eighteenth century, the enemies of the Jesuits, both religious and civilians, argued that the Jesuits were trying to create an independent state within the colonial system.[157] When the Jesuits were expelled from the Iberian world, and finally dissolved by the pope in 1773, the other Catholic orders undertook the task of pacifying the Indian nomads, but they were not very successful.

In the beginning, the church depended for its maintenance mostly on royal subsidies, tithes, and private donations. But gradually it became involved in banking, entrepreneurial administration, mining, urban real estate, and agricultural production. By the end of the eighteenth century, the church controlled about fifty percent of the Spanish American agricultural lands. Although these lands had belonged to the Indians, they were acquired indirectly. The lands of the church were mainly donated by Catholic sinners who wanted to ensure salvation in heaven, and many of those lands could not be sold or divided. The *mayorazgo* (entailed estate) was the effort of the upper classes to perpetuate their wealth and social hierarchy with the collaboration of the church. By then, the church had lost its missionary spirit and had become the superopulent institution that even today can be recognized.

By the outset of the eighteenth century, Portugal depended economically on England, and its military security was virtually guaranteed by the British navy. The Treaty of Methuen (1703) forced Portugal to reduce its customs tariffs on British textiles and merchandise in exchange for the preferential treatment of Portuguese wines entering Britain. Between 1690 and 1770, there was an export boom in

Brazilian gold and diamonds. Brazil exported more than one thousand tons of gold during the eighteenth century,[158] and had emerged as the biggest producer of gold in the world. During the eighteenth century, Brazil was responsible for 80 percent of the total gold production in the world. In reality, the Brazilian gold production was higher than the Spanish American production of the two previous centuries.[159] The cultivation of sugarcane and cotton by African slaves constituted major items of Brazilian production, but by the seventeenth century, they had lost competitiveness in international markets. Moreover, Brazilian exports were never restricted to only one or two products. Brazil exported vegetable oils, wax, spices, leather, woods, corn, tobacco, nuts, parrots, and monkeys. However, sugar continued to be the biggest source of foreign income. The Brazilian historian Caio Prado asserts that the colonial economy of his country was fundamentally organized and administered in relation to international demand.[160] Brazil had emerged as the most profitable and important colony of the Portuguese Empire. In 1720, Brazil was promoted from Governorship-General to Viceroyalty.[161] Marquis of Pombal and the Minister of the Portuguese crown (1755–1777) tried to reform and modernize Portugal without too much success. Pombal led an economic proto-nationalism with an enlightened despotism that intended to promote Portuguese industrialization and to improve the administration of Brazil.

The Iberian naval decadence precipitated threats by other European powers, but the Spanish pride and stubbornness rejected any form of British tutelage. With the death of the Hapsburg king Charles II in 1700, France, in its quest to penetrate the rich Spanish American colonies, fought to place a Bourbon on the Spanish throne. After the War of the Spanish Succession (1701–13) and the Peace of Utrecht, Spain was able to keep its American colonies in exchange for concessions to England. The British were allowed an annual direct sale to the colonies of English products and *asientos* (African slaves). With the Bourbon ascent to the Spanish throne, a series of measures were taken in order to promote the modernization of the Spanish Empire. Spain debated how to end the humiliation of being considered the sick man of Europe. With French physiocratic inspiration, industry and agriculture were to be promoted. The contemporary rationalism sanctioned modernization through the applied sciences. The colonies would be granted more economic freedom, but industrialization would remain as a metropolitan priority. Such a project required economic expansion, and the further centralization of the state that conspired against the monopolies of the traditional Spanish and Spanish American elites. Moreover, all the Spanish provinces were to profit from the modernization and the mercantilist expansion.

Despite the Spanish francophobia, the Bourbons introduced in Spain the French *intendant* system in order to improve the tax collections and government policies. However, until the ascent of Charles III (1759–1788), the Bourbon projects were not very successful in Spain or the colonies. Increasingly aggressive English smuggling as well as the English capture of Havana (1762–63), and its use as an entrepôt to smuggle merchandise to the Spanish American colonies, forced the Spanish crown to take more drastic measures for the modernization of the empire. After 1765, several Spanish ports were authorized to trade directly with the main Caribbean ports. Merchant companies from Barcelona, Bilbao, and Zaragoza were assigned part of the colonial markets. Spanish American ports were also opened to intercolonial trade in local products. Thus, the requirement for trading only through the system of armed fleets was gradually eliminated.[162] The fleets were organized by merchants, and they formed guarded marine convoys to protect the privately owned merchandise. Registered ships gradually replaced the fleets. However, the liberalization of trade in Spanish America did not take place without conflicts between the old and new socioeconomic actors.[163]

Mostly because of modernizing policies, there was an increase in Spanish trade with the colonies and also in fiscal revenues. There was a swift growth in the colonial production of silver, gold, sugar, cacao, coffee, cotton, dyes, leather, and tobacco. The liberalization and expansion of trade brought the decline of the House of Trade and the fleet system. However, with the advent of the French Revolution, the Spanish and Portuguese crowns regarded the modernizing projects with fear and began to delay reforms. Moreover, the Bourbon and Portuguese reforms did little or nothing to improve the subhuman living conditions of the unprivileged masses and the Amerindians in particular. While administrative modernization attempted to increase production and fiscal revenues, Bourbon fantasies tried to implant the ideas of progress and the Enlightenment, while the Indian tributes were increased. The ethnic communities that still were ruled through the caciques were afterward subjected to the physical presence of colonial bureaucrats that controlled the collection of tributes and the confiscation of local resources.[164] The Bourbon project required greater sacrifices from the Indians, the slaves, and the least privileged. In the Andean region, bureaucratic reforms generated conflicts among the Indian communities. Endorsing the fantasy of enlightened despotism, Pombal argued that modernization would reach the Indians if they learned Portuguese and their women married White men.

By the end of the Latin American colonial period, the Indians still constituted the most numerous inhabitants. Out of a total of seventeen million people, only three million were Whites. The Indians made up almost eight million, and the rest were castes and Blacks. In Brazil, of a population of three million people, only about five hundred thousand were Whites; fewer than ten percent would remain as pure Indians. Latin American racial heterogeneity as well as fragmentation among the colored masses facilitated the socioeconomic and political hegemony of the Neo-European elites. The Latin American colonial heritage would be one of extreme affluence for the elites and one of extreme misery for the masses. Only at the outset of the third millennium would Amerindians exist in numbers similar to those at the time of Columbus, but whereas they had comprised the majority of the American population, they were now converted to a minority.

The French regicide and anarchy led Spain to suspend relations with France from 1793 to 1796. In the interlude, Spain sought an alliance with England in order to modernize and defend itself, but the British were not interested in modernizing the Spanish navy or the economy. The British took over Trinidad in 1797, and on two occasions attempted to capture Buenos Aires (1806–1807). The British had an interest in smuggling and in penetrating the Iberian American market as well as in obtaining raw materials and specifically precious metals. At a time when trade increased between the criollos and the British, the Spanish crown required more income and loans from the colonies. In 1804, a royal decree of consolidation sequestered the colonial Charity Funds and ordered that they be sent to Spain. Fifteen million pesos were sent to Spain before the hated consolidations were suspended four years later. The Spanish consolidations and disentailments have been considered analogous to the contemporary British enclosures and to the French sale of ecclesiastical properties. Those were sociofiscal processes that promoted the "agrarian economic liberalism."[165] The consolidation was also a monarchical attack against the economic power of the church. However, the financial role of the Spanish American church was much more entrepreneurial than in Spain.

Despite the criollos' resentments against the Spaniards, they looked at the crown as a guarantee against the demands of the unprivileged masses: Indians, Blacks, and castes. Legally, the criollos did not exist because all the Whites were Spanish. The term "criollo" had some depreciatory connotation for the Whites because it implied racial impurity. The criollos preferred to call themselves Spanish Americans. It is the postcolonial historiography that has made them heroes and notable protagonists. The bloody Haitian independence movement (1804) and the Indian rebellions of the eighteenth century inspired a conservative desire for the status quo among the Iberian American elites. In addition, the criollos observed the revolutions in the United States and France. They were quick to consider options that would allow them more free commerce. Above all, the criollos sought corporate freedoms instead of individual liberties. The criollo intellectuals who adopted the slogans of the French Revolution drew upon profound scholastic formation and heritage.[166]

Indian and African slave rebellions occurred from the dawn of the European domination in the New World. But in Haiti, the French Revolution and the Napoleonic Wars favored the emergence of the first Latin American nation-state. Unlike in the Tupac Amaru rebellion, the Haitian slaves confronted a colonial state in crisis. Haiti also became the first African national state in world history as well as the first successful slave revolution of the common era. The Napoleonic invasion of the Iberian Peninsula in 1807, as well as long-held resentments, eventually ignited a passion for emancipation among the Iberian Americans. The resistance against the French invaders was led by the Seville Junta (May–September 1808), which united the Andalucian oligarchy with all its international connections. It was a conservative junta, determined to maintain the corporate and monopolist system with all its errors and privileges. When the Seville Junta was replaced by the Central Junta, the criollos and Indianos became enthusiastic about its promise to liberalize trade. However, the replacement of the Central Junta by the Regency (pro-Fernando) and its flight to Cadiz, where the traditional monopolist interests were the real authority, brought about the emergence of revolutionary juntas in Caracas (April 1810) and Buenos Aires (May 1810). The criollos, like the Indians before them, began their revolutions in the name of the king.

The Spanish elites had three political parties in Cadiz: the Serviles, the Liberals, and the Indianos (Americans). The debates dealt with the struggle against Napoleon and the first European liberal constitution. At least in theory, the Spanish Constitution of 1812 eliminated the Indian tribute and other personal services. Wage earners would replace neofeudal obligations. However, those liberal slogans would only slowly become reality, and through violence during the next two centuries. The Constitutional debaters also discussed the abolition of Black slavery. But Afro-American slavery was not completely abolished until 1888 in Brazil. Amerindian slavery also lasted longest in the Amazon region.

The Indianos of Cadiz and Spain favored monarchical absolutism. Despite their proclaimed loyalty to Fernando VII, the Venezuelan and Argentinean criollos had already sparked the fire of the bloody independence wars that bled Spanish America for more than a decade. It was the criollos at the Spanish American periphery who became the vanguard of emancipation. From the outset, the independence movement became a criollo project despite the fact that many Indians, Blacks, and castes fought and died in response to criollo promises and libertarian illusions. For a number of reasons, more Indians fought on

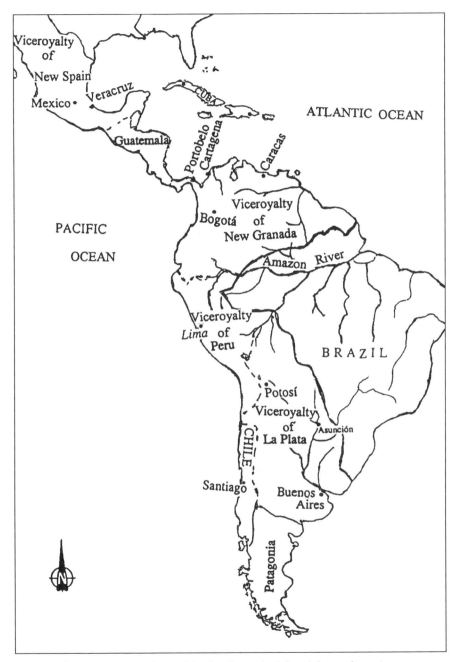

Ibero-American viceroyalties by the end of the eighteenth century.

the side of the crown than with the Liberators at the final battle of Ayacucho (December 9, 1824).[167] In fact, the Indian majorities and the castes from the Peruvian interior sympathized more with the crown than with the criollo patriots.[168] Moreover, the Iquichano Indians (Huanta, Ayacucho) refused to surrender, and fought on the side of their king until they were defeated in 1828. Latin American independence also represented the breakdown of the "colonial pact."[169] Above all, Latin American independence was a movement of political separation from metropolitan powers. Except in the case of the Haitian revolution, there were no drastic social changes; nor were non-Whites and ethnic groups liberated. The colored peoples were the majority of the casualties during the independence wars, but they had no say in ending them.

Latin American independence took place at the time when England preached and supported free trade around the world. Local resentments against the unfairness of the colonial system emerged when the metropolitan powers were in crisis. It was the less oppressed who led the independence movement. They would appropriate for themselves the neophyte national states with all their democratic mythologies, and the nationalisms that flourished afterward. But the Amerindians, castes, and Blacks remain as the most exploited and excluded in Latin America. Latin Americanism remains a concept that has not been completely assimilated by the majority of Latin Americans. It is mostly when people from south of the Rio Grande go abroad that they are reminded about their Latin American identity.

Toward a History of the Amerindian Civilizations

1. Luis G. Lumbreras, *La arqueología como ciencia social* (Lima, 1974), 14-16. See also: Miguel León-Portilla, *Los antiguos mexicanos a través de sus crónicas y cantares* (México, D.F., 1961).
2. Bartolomé de Las Casas, "A Very Brief Relation of the Destruction of the Indians, 1552," in *The Black Legend*, edited by Charles Gibson (New York, 1969), 75.
3. Lewis U. Hanke, *Aristotle and the American Indians: A Study of Race Prejudice in the Modern World* (London, 1959), 41-42.
4. Richard E. Greenleaf, *Zumarraga and the Mexican Inquisition, 1536-1543* (Washington, D.C., 1962), 27-32.
5. C.R. Boxer, *The Church Militant and Iberian Expansion, 1440-1770* (Baltimore, 1978), 84-91. See also Mario Góngora, *Studies in Colonial History of Spanish America* (London, 1975), 51, 57, 161; Xavier Albó, "Jesuitas y culturas indígenas," *América Indígena* (México, D.F.) 26 (4) (1966): 395-96, 425-26.
6. Gibson, *The Black Legend*, 14.
7. T. D. Stewart, *The People of America* (New York, 1973), 15-17. See also Alfred W. Crosby, *The Columbian Exchange* (Westport, Conn., 1976), 30.
8. Paul Rivet, *Les origins de l'homme americain* (Paris, 1957). See also A.A. Mendes Correa, "O significado genealógico do 'australopithecus' e do cranio de tabgha e o arco antrofilético índico," *Trabalhos sociales portugueses antropológicos* 2 (3) (1925): 249-86.
9. David M. Hopkins (ed.), *The Bering Land Bridge* (Stanford, 1967).
10. The Argentinean scientist Florentino Ameghino (1854-1911) was the most famous defender of this theory.
11. The American archeologist Anna Roosevelt of the Museum of Natural History (Chicago) is the most famous defender of this theory.
12. Today's commercial cottons originate mostly from cottons cultivated by Amerindians. E. Bradford Burns, *Latin America: A Concise Interpretive History*, 3rd ed. (Englewood Cliffs, N.J., 1982), 17.
13. Ignacio Bernal, *Mexico Before Cortez* (New York, 1975), 11-16. See also Charles B. Heiser, *Seed to Civilization* (San Francisco, 1973), xi, 5-12.
14. L. S. Stavrianos, *The World to 1500* (Englewood Cliffs, N.J., 1982), 337-38.
15. Tzvetan Todorov, *The Conquest of America* (New York, 1985), 84.
16. Jonathan Haas, *The Evolution of the Prehistoric State* (New York, 1982), 1-16, 86-152, 208-17.
17. Mexicans also had a similar concept, called Cihuacoatl.
18. The lowest figure has been proposed by the Argentinean Angel Rosenblat, while the highest number has been defended by the American historian Woodrow Borah and the so-called Berkeley School. Angel Rosenblat, *La población indígena de América desde 1492 hasta la actualidad* (Buenos Aires, 1945). See also Woodrow Borah and Sherburne F. Cook, *The Aboriginal Population of Central Mexico on the Eve of the Spanish Conquest* (Berkeley, 1963).

19. Guillermo Céspedes, *Latin America: The Early Years* (New York, 1974), 49.

20. See the demographic figures in this book in the discussion of high cultures.

21. Before the English colonization of North America, the great population centers of the Mississippi culture would have been decimated through plagues brought by Spanish explorers. Crosby, *Ecological Imperialism* (Cambridge, U.K., 1993), 210-15. See also Lynda Saffer, *Native Americans Before 1492* (New York, 1992).

22. Alfred Kidder II, "South American Penetrations in Middle America," in *The Maya and Their Neighbors*, edited by Clarence L. Hay et al. (New York, 1977), 441-59. Precious stones from Brazil have also been found in Peru. See the collection in the Museo de Oro (Lima, Peru). This museum belongs to the Mújica Gallo family.

23. Edmundo Guillén, *Versión inca de la conquista* (Lima, 1974).

24. Frederick Peterson, *Ancient Mexico* (New York, 1962), 40. My friend and colleague Magnus Mörner has suggested to me that the phenotypes found in archeological remains could also be Australoids. I agree with such a possibility.

25. J. Alden Mason, *The Ancient Civilization of Peru* (New York, 1971). See also: Dennis Lou, "The Mesoamerican 'Mushroom Stones' and the Chinese Ancestor Tablets," *XXXVI Congreso internacional de americanistas: Actas y memorias*, vol. 1 (Madrid, 1964), 91.

26. Joseph Campbell, *Oriental Mythology: The Masks of God* (New York, 1991), 398-401.

27. Cyrus Gordon, *Before Columbus* (London, 1971). See also: A. Hyatt Verrill and Ruth Verrill, *America's Ancient Civilizations* (New York, 1967).

28. Helge Ingstad, "Norse Explorers and Norse Sites at L'Anse Aux Meadows," in *The Quest for America*, edited by Geoffrey Ashe et al. (New York, 1971), 96-112, 175-96.

29. Paul Shao, *Asiatic Influences in Pre-Columbian Art* (Ames, Iowa, 1976).

30. Thor Heyerdahl, *Sjövägarna till Polynesien* (Stockholm, 1967), 68, 81.

31. Samples of such pottery can be found at the Museo Arqueológico Rafael Larco (Lima, Peru).

32. Lou, "Chinese Inscriptions Found in Pre-Columbian objects," *XXXVII Congreso internacional de americanistas: Actas y memorias*, vol. 4 (Buenos Aires, 1968), 179-184. See also Song Boozhong and Wang Dayaou, "Antiguas relaciones entre China y Perú," *Debate* (Buenos Aires) 7 (24) (October–November 1994): 46-49.

33. Jorge E. Hardoy, *Pre-Columbian Cities* (London, 1973), 364, 381-84. Chan Chan and the adjacent areas still have not been properly explored by Western scholars. Professor Alberto Pinillos Rodríguez, historian at the Universidad Nacional de Trujillo (Peru), is the academic with the greatest understanding of this pre-Columbian metropolis.

34. Interview with Professor Tomohiro Takayama, Sofia University (October 26, 1983, Tokyo, Japan).

35. R. C. Padden, *The Hummingbird and the Hawk* (New York, 1967), 28.

36. León-Portilla, *Pre-Columbian Literature of Mexico* (Norman, Okla., 1969), 60.

37. Bernal Díaz, *The Conquest of New Spain*, translated by J. M. Cohen (Baltimore, 1963), 123.

38. Julio C. Tello, *Wira-Kocha* (Lima, 1923). Dragon figures have also been observed in Central America. Samuel K. Lothrop, "Peruvian Stylistic Impact on Lower Central America," in *Essays in Pre-Columbian Art and Archeology*, edited by Lothrop et al. (Cambridge, Mass., 1961), 261.

39. Pedro Sarmiento de Gamboa, *History of the Incas* (Cambridge, U.K., 1907), 32, 186. See also Heyerdahl, *Early Man and the Ocean* (London, 1978), 179.

40. *Fakta* (Oslo), May 1988, 8.

41. Inca Garcilaso de la Vega, *Comentarios reales de los Incas* (Lima, 1973): vol. 1, 172-73; vol. 2, 152-53.

42. Helene Martinsson-Wallin, *Ahu—The Ceremonial Stone Structures of Easter Island*, Societas Archeologica Upsaliensis, Aun 19 (Uppsala, 1994).
43. Samuel Eliot Morison (ed.), *Journals and Other Documents on the Life and Voyages of Christopher Columbus* (New York, 1963), 74.
44. Hernán Cortés, *Cartas de relación de la conquista de México*, 6th ed., Colección Austral (Madrid, 1979), 220.
45. Morison, *Journals*, 374-75.
46. Interview with Professors Wu Tai and Chen Kao-hua, History Institute, Peking University (July 10, 1981, Peking, China).
47. Donald H. Keith and Christian J. Buys, "New Light on Medieval Chinese Seagoing Ship Construction," *The International Journal of Nautical Archeology* 10 (2) (May 1981), 119-32. See also "Till sjöss och på land," *Kina rapport* 3 (Stockholm, 1980), 21-25.
48. Arnold Pacey, *Technology in World Civilization, a Thousand-Year History* (Cambridge, U.K., 1990), 162-63. See also Joseph Needham, *Clerks and Craftsmen in China and the West* (Cambridge, U.K., 1970), 41, 48, 52. When Vasco Da Gama arrived at Calcutta in 1498, the Portuguese Caravels weighed at the most 300 tons.
49. W. E. Cheong, "Historia de un abandono," *El correo de la UNESCO* (August-September, 1991): 20-23.
50. The Colombian historian Gustavo Vargas Martínez of the Universidad Autónoma de México is the scholar with the most extensive knowledge of sources related to Chinese-Amerindian contacts.
51. Interview with Professors Kobayashi Kazuhiro and Tomohiro Takayama, Sofia University (October 26, 1983), Tokyo, Japan.
52. George I. Quimby, "Culture Contact on the Northwest Coast, 1785-1795," *American Anthropologist* 50 (2) (June 1948): 247-55.
53. Betty J. Meggers, "Contacts from Asia," in *The Quest for America*, edited by Ashe, 242.
54. Meggers, Clifford Evans, and Emilio Estrada, *Early Formative Period of Coastal Ecuador: The Valdivia and Machialilla Phases* (Washington, D.C., 1965), 158.
55. Meggers, "The Transpacific Origin of Mesoamerican Civilization," *American Anthropologist* 77 (1) (March 1975): 1-27.
56. The Western conception of three human races goes back to Genesis. The three sons of Noah, who survived the Great Flood, Shem, Ham, and Jafet, would be the founders of the three races.
57. See among others, Eric Von Daniken, *Chariots of Gods* (New York, 1971). See also Alan and Sally Landsburg, *The Outer Space Connection* (New York, 1975).
58. Peterson, *Ancient Mexico*, 9.
59. Diego de Landa, *Relación de las cosas de Yucatán*, edited by A. M. Tozzer (Cambridge, Mass., 1941).
60. Las Casas, *History of the Indies*, edited by Andrew Collard (New York, 1971), xii.
61. Inga Clendinnen, *Ambivalent Conquests: Maya and Spaniard in Yucatán, 1517-1570* (New York, 1987), 165, 182.
62. A French Franciscan, who lived for several years among the Tupinamba of Brazil in the sixteenth century, discovered that those Indians also believed in an omnipresent and omnipotent god called Nonan. See André Thevet, "La cosmographie universelle," in *Les français en Amérique pendant la deuxième moité de XVIe siècle: le Brésil et les bresiliens*, edited by Suzanne Lussagnet (Paris, 1953), 37-38.
63. C. A. Burland, *The Gods of Mexico* (New York, 1968).
64. Padden, *The Hummingbird and the Hawk*.
65. Peterson, *Ancient Mexico*, 146.
66. Morison, *Journals*, 146.

67. For a subtle theory about cannibalistic liturgy, see Hans Becher, "Endocaniba-lismo Yanonámi," *XXXVII Congreso internacional de americanistas: Actas y memorias*, vol. 3 (Buenos Aires, 1968), 41-49.

68. Michael E. Smith, "Life in the Provinces of the Aztec Empire," *Scientific American* 270 (September 1997), 58.

69. Stewart, *The People of America*, 79-80.

70. Heiser, *Seed to Civilization*, 24.

71. Marvin Harris, *Cows, Pigs, Wars and Witches* (New York, 1974), 178.

72. Enrique Florescano, "Una nueva Historia de los Mayas," *América Indígena* (México, D.F.), 50 (1) (January-March 1990): 151.

73. Richard E. W. Adamas (ed.), *The Origins of Maya Civilization* (Albuquerque, New Mexico, 1977). See also Norman Hamond and Gordon P. Wiley, *Maya Archeology and Ethno-History* (Austin, Tex., 1979).

74. Carlos J. Lettner, "Las escrituras americanas," *Anuario Indigenista* 33 (December 1973): 87-154. See also Joyce Marcus, "Zapotec Writing," *Scientific American* 242 (February 1980): 46-60.

75. Y. V. Knórozov, *Códices jeroglíficos de los Mayas* (Leningrad, 1975).

76. Michael D. Coe, *Breaking the Maya Code* (London, 1992), 32.

77. Paul Arnold, *El libro maya de los muertos* (México, D.F., 1990), 9-18, 25.

78. David Stuart and Stephen D. Houston, "Maya Writing," *Scientific American* 261 (August 1989): 75.

79. Beatriz de la Fuente, *Los hombres de Piedra: Escultura Olmeca* (México, D.F., 1977).

80. Adams, *The Origins of Maya Civilization*, 383-423.

81. Entrepreneurial shamans also emerged in the Central American isthmus. See Mary W. Helms, *Ancient Panama: Chiefs in Search of Power* (Austin, Tex., 1979).

82. Alfred M. Tozzer, "Landa's Relation de las Cosas de Yucatán," *Papers of the Peabody Museum of American Archeology and Ethnology*, vol. 18 (Cambridge, Mass., 1941), 96-97.

83. Adams, *The Origins of Maya Civilization*, 405.

84. Lothrop, "South America as Seen from Middle America," 427-29.

85. For a synthesis of Boole's vigesimal algebra, see Olof Eriksson, *Autoteleteknik*, 3rd ed. (Stockholm, 1969), 5-33.

86. Raymond Van Over (ed.), *I Ching* (New York, 1971), xi-444.

87. *Popol Vuh*, edited by Adrián Recinos (México, D.F., 1994), 105.

88. Robert Wauchope, "Late Horizons of Maya Prehistory," in *The Indian Background of Latin American History*, edited by Wauchope (New York, 1970), 99.

89. Vernon L. Scarbough and Gary G. Gallopin, "A Water Storage in the Maya Lowlands," *Science* 251 (4994) (February 1991): 658-62.

90. Amalia Atloloni Lecón, "El maya, su esclavitud y su comercio," *Memoria del congreso conmemorativo del X aniversario del Departamento de Etnohistoria*, Cuaderno de trabajo No. 4, Instituto nacional de antropología e historia (México, D.F., 1988), 107-20.

91. Cited in *Problems in Latin American Civilization: Indian Labor in the Spanish Indies*, edited by Francis Bannon (Boston, 1966), 5.

92. Linda Schele and David Freidel, *A Forest of Kings: The Untold Story of the Ancient Maya* (New York, 1990).

93. "Torka utrotade mayafolket," *Illustrated Vetenskap* 13 (December 1996): 23.

94. Robert Sharer, "The Maya Collapse Revisited: Internal and External Perspectives," in *Social Process in Maya Prehistory*, edited by Norman Hamond (Baltimore, 1977), 531-52.

95. Nicholas Georgescu-Rogen, *Energy and Economic Myths: Institutional and Analytical Economic Essays* (New York, 1976), 6.

96. Colin A. Ronan, *The Cambridge Illustrated History of the World's Science* (London, 1983), 51.
97. Bernal, *Mexico Before Cortez*, 57-59.
98. Peterson, *Ancient Mexico*, 67-69.
99. León-Portilla, *De besegrades version* (Stockholm, 1971), 8.
100. Rudolf van Zantwijk, "El origen de la sociedad y el estado azteca así como la historicidad de las fuentes autóctonas, una introducción," *Boletín de estudios latinoamericanos y del Caribe* (Amsterdam) 18 (June 1975): 4-14.
101. Maarten Jansen, "La serpiente emplumada y el amanecer de la historia," in *Códices y comunidades*, edited by Maarten Jansen and Luis Reyes García (Leiden, Holland, 1997), 25.
102. Tenochtitlán emerged as the dominating metropolis due to an alliance with the cities of Texcoco and Tlacopán in 1430. Edward E. Calnek, "Patterns of Empire Formation in the Valley of Mexico," in *The Inca and the Aztec States, 1400-1800*, edited by George A. Collier et al. (New York, 1982), 56.
103. Pedro Armillas, "The Way to Empire: The Aztec," in *The Indian Background of Latin American History*, 50. See also Borah and Cook, *The Aboriginal Population of Central Mexico on the Eve of the Spanish Conquest.*
104. The best descriptions of the city were written by Bernal Díaz del Castillo, Hernán Cortés, and López de Gómara.
105. Pedro Carrasco, "Some Theoretical Considerations about the Role of the Market in Ancient Mexico," *Economic Anthropology*, edited by Sutti Ortiz (Lanham, Md., 1983), 67-82.
106. Stanley J. Stein and Barbara H. Stein, *The Colonial Heritage of Latin America* (New York, 1970), 33.
107. Charles Gibson, *The Aztecs under Spanish Rule* (Stanford, 1964), 5.
108. H. R. Harvey and B. J. Williams, "Aztec Arithmetic: Positional and Area Calculation," *Science* 210 (31) (October 1980): 499-505.
109. Juan Batalla Rosado, "El palacio real mexica," en *Códices, caciques y comunidades*, edited by Jansen and Reyes García, 65-97.
110. Gibson, "The Aztec Aristocracy in Colonial Mexico," *Comparative Studies in Society and History*, vol. 2 (1959-1960), 169-170. See also J. Rounds, "Dynastic Succession and the Centralization in Tenochtitlan," in *The Inca and Aztec States, 1400-1800*, 63-84.
111. Fernando Díaz Infante, *La educación de los Aztecas* (México, D.F., 1988), 36-37.
112. Burr C. Brundage, *Two Earths, Two Heavens: An Essay Contrasting the Aztecs and the Incas* (Albuquerque, N. Mex., 1975).
113. López de Gómara, *Cortés*, 345-46, 350-54, 362-64.
114. Cortés, *Cartas*, 248.
115. Helms, *Middle America* (Englewood Cliffs, N.J., 1975), 169.
116. Cortés, *Cartas*, 220.
117. Angel María Garibal (ed.), *Vida económica de Tenochtitlán* (México, D.F., 1961), 30-39, 53, 70, 178.
118. Cortés, *Cartas*, 70-71.
119. Munehiro Kobayashi, *Tres estudios sobre el sistema tributario de los Mexicas* (México, D.F., 1993).
120. Gibson, "The Aztec Aristocracy in Colonial Mexico," 170. See also Carrasco, "The Economy of the Aztec and Inca States," in *The Inca and Aztec States, 1400-1800*, 23-39.
121. The best descriptions of courtly life have been written by Bernal Díaz del Castillo, Hernán Cortés, and López de Gómara.
122. John Rowe, "Absolute Chronology in the Andean Area," *American Antiquity* 10 (3) (1945): 265-84.

123. Åke Wedin, *La cronología de la historia incaica* (Madrid, 1963); Wedin, *El concepto de lo incaico* (Uppsala, Sweden, 1966).

124. Magnus Mörner, "Wedin's Work in General," *The Americas* 25 (2) (October 1968): 174-79. See also: Hans Andersson, "One Aspect of Wedin's Work," *The Americas* 25 (2) (October 1968): 180-90.

125. The archeological research by Tokyo University is demonstrating that the age of the Andean culture has even earlier origins. See Seiichi Izumi and Kazuo Terada, *Excavations at Kotosh, Peru* (Tokyo, 1972).

126. Nicolás Sánchez-Albornoz, *The Population of Latin America: A History* (Berkeley, 1974), 34.

127. Henry Dobyns, "Estimating Aboriginal American Population: An Appraisal of Techniques with a New Hemisphere Estimate," *Current Anthropology* 7 (1966): 395-449.

128. Noble D. Cook, *Demographic Collapse: Indian Peru, 1520-1620* (Cambridge, U.K., 1981), 114.

129. Dobyns, "An Outline of Andean Epidemic History to 1720," *Bulletin of the History of Medicine* 37 (6) (1963): 493-515.

130. Waldemar Espinoza Soriano, *La destrucción del imperio de los Incas* (Lima, 1977), 61.

131. Karl Marx, "Zur kritik der politischen oekonomie," in Marx and Friedrich Engels, *Gesammelte Werke*. See also Friedrich Katz, *Ancient American Civilizations* (New York, 1972), 282; Pedro Scarón (ed.), *Karl Marx, Friedrich Engels: Materiales para la historia de América Latina* (México, D.F., 1975), 30.

132. Rosa Luxemburg, *Introducción a la economía* (Madrid, 1974), 114, 118-122.

133. María Rostworowski, *Ensayos de historia andina* (Lima, 1993), 39.

134. Lumbreras, *La arqueología como ciencia social*, 240.

135. Steve Stern, *Peru's Indian Peoples and the Challenge of the Spanish Conquest: Huamanga to 1640* (Madison, Wis., 1982), 8-17, 22-26.

136. Terrence N. D'Altroy, *Provincial Power in the Inka Empire* (Washington, D.C., 1992).

137. Burns, *Latin America: A Concise Interpretive History*, 289.

138. R. Tom Zuidema, *Inca Civilization in Cuzco* (Austin, Tex., 1990), 68, 89-90.

139. Rostworowski, *La mujer en el Perú precolombino*, Documento de trabajo No. 72 (Lima, 1995), 13.

140. Reginaldo de Lizárraga, *Descripción breve de toda la tierra del Perú, Tucumán, Río de la Plata y Chile*, Nueva biblioteca de autores españoles, vol. 15 (Madrid, 1909), 519.

141. J. M. Cohen (ed.), *Zárate: The Discovery and Conquest of Peru* (Baltimore, 1968), 123.

142. The American anthropologist John Murra has extensively explained the noted process.

143. The late Peruvian ethnohistorian Franklin Pease maintained that after the breakup of the Inca Empire, the Ayllu survived during the colonial period. See Franklin Pease, *Del Tawantinsuyo a la historia del Perú* (Lima, 1978).

144. Rostworowski, *Ensayos de historia andina*, 105-106, 110.

145. Hermes Tovar, *Notas sobre el modo de producción precolombino* (Bogotá, 1974), 89-110. See also John Murra, *Formaciones económicas y políticas en el mundo andino* (Lima, 1975).

146. Roger Bartra, *El modo de producción asiático* (México, D.F., 1969), 21-231.

147. Joel Gunn and Richard Adams, "Climatic Change, Culture and Civilization in North America," *World Archaeology* 13 (1) (June 1981): 93.

148. Katz, *The Ancient American Civilizations*.

149. Garcilaso de la Vega, *Comentarios reales de los Incas*, vol. 3, 166.

150. Emilio Harth-Terre and Alberto Márquez Abanto, "El histórico puente sobre el

río Apurimac," *Revista del archivo nacional del Perú* 25 (1961): 1-61.

151. Garcilaso de la Vega, *Comentarios*, vol. 1, 150-51.

152. Cited by Garcilaso de la Vega, *Comentarios*, vol. 3, 165.

153. John Hyslop, *The Inka Road System* (Orlando, Fla., 1984), 2, 247, 254, 341.

154. The chasquis were young men especially trained for their profession; they were stationed in intervals of about 1,500 meters.

155. Juan de Sáamanos, *Relación de los primeros descubrimientos de Francisco Pizarro y Diego de Almagro*, Colección de documentos inéditos para la historia de España, vol. 5 (Madrid, 1844), 196. See also Heyerdahl, *Early Man and the Ocean* (Garden City, N.Y., 1979), 188.

156. A replica of the guara is in the Kon-Tiki Museum (Oslo, Norway).

157. Garcilaso de la Vega, *Comentarios*, vol. 2, 164. See also: E. Frank, "Stone Working in Ancient Peru," *Archaeometry* 22 (2) (1980): 211-12.

158. Heather Lechtman, "Pre-Columbian Surface Metallurgy," *Scientific American* 250 (June 1984): 38-45.

159. Meteoritic iron balls processed by Inca technicians are in the Museo Arqueológico Rafael Larco (Lima, Peru).

160. Alden, *The Ancient Civilizations of Peru*, 167. See also José Alcina Franch and Miguel Dorado, "Exploración arqueológica de la costa de Esmeraldas, Ecuador," *Revista española de antropología americana*, vol. 6 (Madrid, 1971), 129.

161. Rubén Vargas Ugarte, S. J., *Historia general del Perú: Virreynato*, vol. 2 (Lima, 1971), 86-87.

162. Artifacts of *llasca* are in the Museo de la Universidad del Cuzco (Peru).

163. Izumi Shimada and John F. Merkel, "Copper-Alloy Metallurgy in Ancient Peru," *Scientific American* 264 (July 1991): 63, 66.

164. Interview with Dr. Milciades Chávez, professor of Biochemestry, Faculty of Medicine, Universidad Nacional de Trujillo, Peru (July 15, 1978). Interview with the curandero Eduardo Calderón Palomino (1930-1996), March 4, 1982, Trujillo. I have also interviewed several times the curandero Elías Avila (1905-1979), Tarapoto, Peru.

165. Fernando Cabieses, *Dioses y enfermedades: La medicina en el antiguo Perú* (Lima, 1974).

166. "La trepanación peruana se difundió en Centroamérica," *El Comercio* (Lima), July 17, 1982, A-7.

167. *La Prensa* (Lima), July 8, 1978, 3. See also: *El Comercio* (Lima), July 12, 1978, A-7.

168. Jeremy Narby, *La serpiente cósmica: El ADN y los orígenes del saber* (Lima, 1997), 46.

169. Garcilaso de la Vega, *Comentarios*, vol. 1, 116-19.

170. Erland Nordenskiöld, "The Secrets of the Peruvian Quipus," *Comparative Ethnological Studies* (Gothenburg) 6 (1-2) (1925).

171. Garcilaso de la Vega, *Comentarios*, vol. 2, 61-66, 79, 84. See also Luis Baudin, *El imperio socialista de los Incas* (Salta, Argentina, 1970), 201-12.

172. Raúl Porras Barrenechea, *Fuentes históricas peruanas* (Lima, 1945), 109.

173. Díaz, *The Conquest of New Spain*, 91-96.

174. Cohen, *Zárate*, 79.

175. Ibid., 7-14. However, the American historian James Lockhart claims that by the "fluidity" of the signatures by Pizarro's men, it can be deduced that some of them were "functional literates." See James Lockhart, *The Men of Cajamarca* (Austin, Tex., 1972).

176. Víctor Angeles Vargas, *Historia del Cuzco* (Lima, 1978). See also *El Comercio* (Lima), July 1, 1978, 27.

177. Vargas Ugarte, *Historia general*, vol. 2, 230-31.

178. Sarmiento de Gamboa, *History of the Incas*, 200.

179. Garcilaso de la Vega, *Comentarios*, vol. 1, 118.
180. Pedro Cieza de León, *La primera parte de la chrónica del Perú* (Sevilla, 1553), ch. 87.
181. Fernando de Montesinos, *Memorias antiguas e historiales del Perú*, edited by Phillip A. Means (London, 1920).
182. Porras Barrenechea, *Fuentes*, 109–117.
183. Rafael Larco Hoyle, "La escritura mochica sobre pallares," *Revista geográfica americana* (Buenos Aires), 18 (107) (August 1942): 93–103. See also Larco Hoyle, *Los Mochicas* (Lima, 1939).
184. Victoria de la Jara, *Introducción al estudio de la escritura de los Inkas* (Lima, 1975).
185. See for example the two-meter-long stone with glyphs found in the Aclla Wuasi. Museo de Santa Catalina (Cuzco, Peru).
186. Ramiro Matos Mendieta, "El secreto de la Quilca," *El Comercio* (Lima), November 24, 1985, Dominical, 6.
187. William Burns Glynn, "La escritura de los Incas," *Boletín de Lima* 12–14 (May–September 1981): 1–32.
188. Two centuries before the common era, the Hebrews also used a numerical alphabet.
189. Gail Silverman, *El tejido andino: Un libro de sabiduría* (Lima, 1994), 143, 150, 176.

From Colonization to Decolonization

1. Miguel León-Portilla, "Qué es el indigenismo interamericano?," *América Indígena* 26 (4) (1966): 341–59. See also León-Portilla, *De besegrades version* (Stockholm, 1971); Yu Zubriski, *Los incas quechuas* (Moscú, 1979), 40, 138–48; Juan Friede and Benjamin Keen (eds.), *Bartolomé de Las Casas in History* (DeKalb, Ill., 1971), 47–53.
2. Nathan Wachtel, *Los vencidos: Los indios del Perú frente a la conquista 1530–1570* (Madrid, 1976). See also Edmundo Guillén, *Versión inca de la conquista* (Lima, 1974).
3. Samuel Eliot Morison (ed.), *Journals and Other Documents on the Life and Voyages of Christopher Columbus* (New York, 1963), 140–41, 185, 226, 395.
4. Gonzalo Fernández de Oviedo y Valdés, *Natural History of the West Indies*, edited and translated by Sterling Stoudemire (Chapel Hill, N.C., 1959), 13–18.
5. Carl O. Sauer, *The Early Spanish Main* (Berkeley, 1966), 59–66.
6. Morison, *Journals*, 61–65, 77.
7. Ibid., 83, 86.
8. This was a mixture of gold and copper that came from South America.
9. Morison, *Journals*, 132–33, 215.
10. Ibid., 67, 99, 146.
11. Although Columbus has been accused of exaggerating the quantities of gold in Haiti and the Caribbean, it has been calculated that by 1520, the Caribbean yield had at least doubled the total European production of gold. See Guillermo Céspedes, *Latin America: The Early Years* (New York, 1974), 29.
12. Irving Rouse, *The Tainos* (New Haven & London, 1992), 7, 18.
13. Peter Hume and Neil L. Whitehead, *Wild Majesty Encounters with Caribs from Columbus to the Present Day* (Oxford, 1992).
14. R. H. Major (ed.), *Christopher Columbus: Four Voyages to the New World, Letters and Selected Documents* (New York, 1961), 29.
15. Morison, *Journals*, 154, 185–86, 271. See also Friede, "Origenes de la esclavitud

indígena en Venezuela," *América Indígena* 22 (1) (1962): 14.

16. Morison, *Journals*, 248.
17. Ibid., 139, 178.
18. Major, *Christopher Columbus*, 54.
19. Ibid., 46, 51.
20. Rouse, *The Tainos*, 16.
21. Ignacio B. Anzoátegui (ed.), *Cristobal Colón: Los cuatro viajes del almirante y su testamento*, Colección Austral (Madrid, 1980). See also Morison, *Journals*, 184, 236; Major, *Christopher Columbus*, 30.
22. Charles Gibson, *The Aztecs under Spanish Rule* (Stanford, 1964), 353.
23. Inca Garcilaso de la Vega, *Comentarios reales de los incas*, vol. 3, Biblioteca Peruana (Lima, 1973), 168-73. See also Ignacio Bernal, *Mexico Before Cortez:Art, History and Legend* (New York, 1975), 126-27; J. Jorge Klor de Alva, "Martín Ocelotl," in *Struggle and Survival*, edited by David Sweet and Gary Nash (Berkeley, 1981), 128-41.
24. Cristobal Colón, *Diario de navegación y otros escritos*, Biblioteca de clásicos dominicanos (Santo Domingo, 1988), 124-125.
25. Similarly, when the Portuguese visited Brazil for the first time in 1500, they did not find cannibalism.
26. Morrison, *Journals*, 100, 103, 117, 212.
27. Simone Dreyfus, "Historical and Political Inter-Connections," in *Themes in Political Organization: The Caribs and their Neighbors*, edited by Audrey B. Colson and H. Dieter Heinen, *Antropológica* (Caracas, 1983-84), 49.
28. William Arens, *The Man-Eating Myth* (Oxford, 1979).
29. Francisco López de Gómara, *Cortés: The Life of the Conqueror by his Secretary*, translated by Lesley Bird Simpson (Berkeley, 1966), 234.
30. Morris Bishop, *The Odyssey of Cabeza de Vaca* (New York, 1933).
31. Manuel García Soriano, *El conquistador español del siglo XVI* (Tucumán, Argentina, 1954), 18.
32. Royal commissions debated the moral aspects of white behavior toward the Indians at Burgos and Valladolid (1512-1513), resulting in a number of laws that included the Requerimiento. Every conquistador was to carry a copy of the Requerimiento to be read aloud before slave raids or battles took place. It contained a history of the world's creation and the holy virtues of Christianity and the Spanish monarchy. Indian refusal resulted in coercive subjugation and an excuse to conduct a "just war."
33. Patricia Seed, "'Are These Not Also Men?': The Indians' Humanity for Spanish Civilization," *Journal of Latin American Studies* 25 (3) (October 1993): 629-52.
34. Bernal Díaz del Castillo, *The True History of the Conquest of Mexico*, facsimile edition (La Jolla, Calif., 1979), 138.
35. Gómara, *Cortés*, 23.
36. Although the Aztec merchants were growing in wealth, they were strictly controlled by the state. Among the Mayas, it was a custom to choose rulers from the most prosperous merchants. See Gómara, *Cortés*, 354, 144-45. See also Alfred M. Tozzer, "Landa's Relación de las cosas de Yucatán," *Papers of the Peabody Museum of American Archeology and Ethnology*, vol. 18 (Cambridge, Mass., 1941), 96-97.
37. The Lord of Chincha (Peru) had thousands of sea vessels for fishing and trade.
38. Hernán Cortés, *Cartas de relación de la conquista de México*, Colección Austral (Madrid, 1979), 21.
39. Bernal Díaz, *The Conquest of New Spain*, translated by J. M. Cohen (Baltimore, 1967), 54, 60.
40. Ross Hassig, *Mexico and the Spanish Conquest* (London, 1994), 54, 60.

41. Díaz del Castillo, *The True History of the Conquest of Mexico*, 57.
42. Pablo Macera, *Historia del Perú: La colonia*, vol. 2 (Lima, 1985), 37.
43. Hernán Horna, "A propósito del descubrimiento asiático de América," *América Indígena* (México, D.F.) 52 (1-2) (January-June 1992): 275-301.
44. Francis J. Brooks, "Motecuzoma Xocoyotl, Hernán Cortés and Bernal Díaz del Castillo: The Construction of an Arrest," *The Hispanic American Historical Review* 75 (2) (May 1995): 178. See also Susan D. Gillespie, *The Aztec Kings: The Construction of Rulership in Mexican History* (Tucson, Ariz., 1989), 231-35.
45. Díaz del Castillo, *The True History of the Conquest of Mexico*, 152-55.
46. The *Códice Florentino* is pictographically illustrated and written in Spanish and Nahua. This document was directed and edited by the Franciscan friar Bernardino de Sahagún. The original copy is in the Medicea-Lorenziana Library (Florence, Italy).
47. Díaz del Castillo, *The True History of the Conquest of Mexico*, 165-66.
48. Ibid., 138.
49. Hassig, *Mexico and the Spanish Conquest*, 63, 88.
50. Fernando de Alva Ixtlilxóchitl, *Obras históricas de Don Fernando de Alva Ixtlilxóchitl*, vol. 1 (México, D.F., 1965), 450-51.
51. Díaz del Castillo, *The True History of the Conquest of Mexico*, 137.
52. Andrés de Tapia, "Relación sobre la conquista de México," in *Colección de documentos para la historia de México*, edited by Joaquín García Icazbalceta, vol. 2 (México, 1866), 554-94.
53. Gómara, *Cortés*, 141-42, 294.
54. John Hemming, *The Conquest of the Incas* (New York, 1970), 34-35.
55. Cortés, *Cartas*, 58. See also Díaz, *The Conquest*, 223-24.
56. David B. Quinn (ed.), *New American World: A Documentary History of North America to 1612*, vol. 2 (New York, 1979), 112, 130, 139-41.
57. Gibson, "The Aztec Aristocracy in Colonial Mexico," *Compartive Studies in Society and History* 2 (1959-60): 174.
58. Sección Histórica, Serie Corregimiento, Sub-serie: Protección de Naturales, Criminal, Año 1636, Año 1759 (Archivo Departamental de Cajamarca, Peru).
59. María Rostworwski, *Pachacamac y el señor de los milagros: Una trayectoria milenaria* (Lima, 1992), 132, 141-43.
60. Manuel Abad y Queipo, "Estado moral y político en que se hallaba la población del virreynato de la Nueva España en 1799," in *Obras Sueltas*, edited by José María Lucio Mora, vol. 1 (Paris, 1837), 54-68. See also Troy S. Floyd (ed.), *The Bourbon Reformers and Spanish Civilization* (Boston, 1966), 19.
61. Gibson (ed.), *The Spanish Tradition in America* (New York, 1968), 86.
62. Garcilaso de la Vega, *Comentarios*, vol. 1, 24, 29, 32-39.
63. Donald Brand, *Geographical Explorations by the Spanish and the Portuguese*, Institute of Latin American Studies of the University of Texas at Austin [1967], 119-20. Offprint Series, No. 43.
64. Rubén Vargas Ugarte, S. J., *Historia general del Perú*, vol. 1 (Lima, 1971), 20-21, 34.
65. J. H. Cohen (ed.), *The Discovery and Conquest of Peru* (Baltimore, 1968), 71. See also Raúl Porras Barrenechea (ed.), *Relación del descubrimiento del reyno del Perú que hizo Diego de Trujillo* (Sevilla, Spain, 1948).
66. Rostworwski, *Doña Francisca Pizarro* (Lima, 1989), 85-86.
67. Velásquez was the conqueror and governor of Cuba.
68. Juan José Vega, *La guerra de los viracochas*, Colección Biblioteca Peruana (Lima, 1963), 8, 11, 20, 35, 51.
69. For the controversy between a historian and an archeologist on whether Huayna Capac died one year earlier or one year later, see: Åke Wedin, *La*

cronología de la historia incaica: Estudio crítico (Madrid, 1963), 15-17, 25-37. See also John Rowe, "Absolute Chronology in the Andean Area," *American Antiquity* 10 (3) (1945): 265-84.

70. John Murra, *La organización económica del Estado inca* (México, D.F., 1989), 16-17. See also Rowe, "Inca Culture at the Time of the Spanish Conquest," in *Handbook of South American Indians*, vol. 2, edited by Julian Steward (Washington, D.C., 1946), 183-330.

71. Julio C. Tello, *Las edades en el Perú por Guamán Poma*, Museo de Antropología (Lima, 1939), 31.

72. Cohen, *Zárate*, 76-79.

73. Ibid., 92-93.

74. This story was written by the chroniclers. It was dramatized by the American historian William H. Prescott, and it is still repeated. See for example Hemming, *The Conquest of the Incas*, 40-45.

75. Antonine Tibesar, *Franciscan Beginnings in Colonial Peru* (Washington, D.C., 1953), 5-6.

76. Pedro Pizarro, *Relación del descubrimiento y conquista de los reinos del Perú*, Biblioteca de Autores Españoles, vol. 168 (Madrid, 1965).

77. James Lockhart, *The Men of Cajamarca: A Social and Biographical Study of the First Conquerors of Peru* (Austin, Tex., 1972), 90, 205-206, 459-63.

78. "Letter from Gaspar de Gárate to Martín de Gárate, Cajamarca, July 20, 1533," in *Letters and People of the Spanish Indies: The Sixteenth Century*, edited by Lockhart and Enrique Otte (London, 1976), 1-3.

79. Macera, *Historia del Perú: La colonia*, vol. 2, 36.

80. Vega, *La guerra*, 100, 113.

81. Martín de Murúa, *Historia general del Perú y descendencia de los incas*, edited by Manuel Ballesteros Gaibrois, vol. 1 (Madrid, 1962), 247-50.

82. De Murúa, *Historia general*, 225-56, 264-65.

83. Gibson, *Tlaxcala in the Sixteenth Century*, 2nd ed. (Stanford, 1967). See also Steve J. Stern, "The Rise and Fall of Indian and White Alliances," *The Hispanic American Historical Review* 61 (3) (August 1981): 461-91.

84. Stern, *Peru's Indian Peoples and the Challenge of the Spanish Conquest: Huamanga to 1640* (Madison, Wis., 1982). See also Jonathan Hass, *The Evolution of the Prehistoric State* (New York, 1982).

85. Dreyfus, "Historical and Political Inter-connections," 47-48.

86. See for example Jack D. Forbes, *Apache, Navaho and Spaniard* (Norman, Okla., 1994).

87. This traditional line of thinking is expressed by the American historian Woodrow Borah. See Borah, *Early Colonial Trade and Navigation between Mexico and Peru* (Berkeley, 1954), 2. For the pre-Columbian trade in the Panama region, see Mary W. Helms, *Ancient Panama: Chiefs in Search of Power* (Austin, Tex., 1979). See also José Alcina Franch and Miguel Rivera Dorado, "Exploración arqueológica en la costa de Esmeraldas, Ecuador," *Revista española de antropología americana* 6 (1971): 130-34. For a description of the markets in the Pacific coast of the Panama-Nicaragua as told by the Indians to Columbus, see Morison, *Journals*, 374.

88. This typical Aztec symbol is in the collection of the Museo Arqueológico Casinelli (Trujillo, Peru).

89. Alfred Kidder II, "South American Penetrations in Middle America," in *The Maya and Their Neighbors*, edited by Clarence L. Hay et al. (New York, 1977), 441-59. Pre-Columbian Caribbean pearls have been found in Peru. See the collection in the Museo de Oro (Lima, Peru).

90. Joseph A. Gagliano, *Coca Prohibition in Peru: The Historical Debates* (Tucson, Arizona, 1994), pp. 22, 27-28.

91. Louise Stark, "Maya-Yunga-Chipayan: A New Linguistic Alignment," *International Journal of American Linguistics* 37 (2) (1972): 119-35.

92. Juan de Sáamano, *Relación de los primeros descubrimientos de Francisco Pizarro y Diego de Almagro*, Colección de documentsos inéditos para la historia de España, vol. 5 (Madrid, 1844), 196. See also Thor Heyerdahl, *Early Man and the Ocean* (New York, 1979), 185, 188, 228.

93. Jorge Marcos, "De ida y vuelta a Acapulco con mercaderes de mullu," in *Arqueología de la costa ecuatoriana*, edited by Jorge Marcos (Quito, 1986), 164-75.

94. Frank Salomon, "A North Andean Trader Complex under Inca Rule," *Ethnohistory* 24 (2) (1987): 63-77.

95. Real Hacienda (1567-1820), Legajo 125, Expediente 31, folios 1-17. Gradually the guilds of Spanish pilots were able to obtain the prohibition of Indian sailors in the Pacific high seas. See Real Hacienda (1684), Legajo 126, Expediente 54, folios 1-8. Archivo Regional La Libertad, Trujillo, Peru.

96. Cortés, *Cartas*, 213, 248.

97. Patrick O'Brien, "European Economic Development: The Contribution of the Periphery," *The Economic History Review* 35 (1) (February 1982): 1-18. After all his statistical calculations and extrapolations, O'Brien concludes that the periphery contributed only by 7 percent annually to the metropolitan economic growth.

98. Pierre Chanu, *Historia cuantitativa, historia serial* (México, D.F., 1987), 107.

99. Eric R. Wolfe, *Europe and the People Without History* (Berkeley, 1997), 255. Spanish American silver was used as a medium of exchange in China until 1935. See Dun J. Li, *The Ageless Chinese* (New York, 1965), 504-505.

100. Rollie E. Poppino, *Brazil: Land and People* (New York, 1968), 40-112. See also Alexander Marchant, *From Barter to Slavery* (Baltimore, 1941).

101. Robert Anderson, "The Quilombos of Palmares," *Journal of Latin American Studies* 28 (3) (October 1996): 559.

102. Fernand Braudel, *The Wheels of Commerce: Civilization and Capitalism, 15th-18th Century*, vol. 2 (New York, 1979), 211, 244.

103. Stuart B. Schwartz, *Sovereignty and Society in Colonial Brazil* (Berkeley, 1973), 14, 362.

104. Real Hacienda (1786), Causas Ordinarias, Legajo 129, Expediente 110, folios 1-8. Archivo Regional La Libertad.

105. Sección Histórica, Legajo 24, Expediente 365, Año 1633, Archivo Departamental de Cajamarca, Peru.

106. Carlos Contreras, *Los mineros y el Rey, los Andes del Norte: Hualgayoc 1770-1825*, Serie Estudios Históricos 16 (Lima, 1995), 88.

107. Guillermo Cespedés, *Latin America: The Early Years* (New York, 1974), 27.

108. Vargas Ugarte, *Historia general del Perú*, vol. 2, 206.

109. Carlos Sempat Assadourian, "The Colonial Economy: The Transfer of the European System of Production," *Journal of Latin American Studies* 24 (Quincentenary Supplement) (1992): 65.

110. Vargas Ugarte, *Historia general del Perú*, vol. 3, 406.

111. Fernando Silva Santisteban, *Los obrajes en el virreynato del Perú* (Lima, 1964), 90.

112. Ibid., 17.

113. Irene Silverblatt, *Moon, Sun, and Witches* (Princeton, 1987), 159, 169, 175, 208.

114. Gibson, *The Aztecs under Spanish Rule*, 220-36.

115. Jorge Juan and Antonio de Ulloa, *A Voyage to South America* (New York, 1964), 158.

116. Nicolás Sánchez-Albornoz, *La población de América Latina desde los tiempos*

precolombinos hasta el año 2000 (Madrid, 1977), 107-10, 122.

117. E. Bradford Burns, *A History of Brazil* (New York, 1980), 17.

118. Francois Chevalier, *Land and Society in Colonial Mexico: The Great Hacienda* (Berkeley, 1963).

119. B. H. Slicher Van Bath, *Real hacienda y economía en Hispanoamérica, 1541-1820* (Amsterdam, 1989).

120. Immanuel Wallerstein, *The Modern World-System II: Mercantilism and the Consolidation of the European World Economy* (New York, 1980), 176. See also Jean Piel, *Capitalisme agraire au Pérou* (Paris, 1975), 150-51.

121. Murdo J. Macleod, *Spanish Central America* (Berkeley, 1973), 325-27. See also W. George Lovell, *Conquest and Survival in Colonial Guatemala* (Montreal, 1985), 174-75.

122. Santos Atahualpa and Tupac Amaru II were educated by the Jesuits.

123. Alberto Flores Galindo, *Aristocracia y plebe: Lima, 1760-1830* (Lima, 1984), 234-35.

124. Robert G. Keith (ed.), *Haciendas and Plantations in Latin American History* (New York, 1977), 10-13.

125. Kathryn Burns, "Gender and the Politics of Mestizaje," *The Hispanic American Historical Review* 78 (1) (February 1998): 34.

126. Magnus Mörner, *Race Mixure in the History of Latin America* (Boston, 1967), 26.

127. Mörner, *La corona española y los foráneos en los pueblos de indios de América* (Stockholm, 1970), 75, 105-106.

128. Verónica Salles-Reese, "Las divergencias semióticas y el proceso de mestizaje en el Perú colonial," *Colonial Latin American Review* 5 (1) (June 1996): 57.

129. Robert G. Keith, *Conquest and Agrarian Change: The Emergence of the Hacienda System on the Peruvian Coast* (Cambridge, Mass., 1976), 101-102.

130. Jacques Lafaye, *Quetzalcóatl and Guadalupe: The Formation of the Mexican National Consciousness, 1531-1813*, translated by Benjamin Keen (Chicago, 1979).

131. William B. Taylor, *Drinking, Homicide, and Rebellion in Colonial Mexican Villages* (Stanford, 1979).

132. Flores Galindo, *Aristocracia y plebe: Lima 1760-1830*, 235.

133. Frederick P. Bowser, *El esclavo africano en el Perú colonial, 1524-1650* (México, D.F., 1977), 402.

134. Leon G. Campbell, *The Military and Society in Colonial Peru, 1750-1810* (Philadelphia, 1978), 36-40, 129-41. See also Ordenazas del Corregidor de Cajamarca . . . para combatir cualquier movimiento de Túpac Amaru, Serie: Corregimiento/Ordinarias, Legajo No. 150, 1781, folios 1-8. Archivo Departamental de Cajamarca.

135. In March 1815, the Maranganí Indians (Tinta, Cuzco) captured Pumacahua and handed him over to the royal army.

136. Flores Galindo, *Buscando un Inca: Identidad y utopía en los Andes* (Havana, 1986).

137. Michael J. Sallnow, *Pilgrims of the Andes: Regional Cults in Cuzco* (Washington, D.C., 1987), 81.

138. Felipe Guamán Poma de Ayala, *El primer nueva corónica y buen gobierno*, vol. 2, edited by Murra and Rolena Adorno (México, D.F., 1980), 511.

139. José Matos Mar, *Yanaconaje y reforma agraria en el Perú* (Lima, 1976), 16-36.

140. See for example, Stern (ed.), *Resistance, Rebellion and Consciousness in the Andean Peasant World, 18th to 20th Centuries* (Madison, Wis., 1987).

141. Doris M. Ladd, *The Mexican Nobility at Independence, 1780-1826* (Austin, Tex., 1976), 25, 184-86.

142. Mörner, *The Andean Past: Land, Societies and Conflicts* (New York, 1985), 98.
143. Mörner et al., "Comparative Approaches to Latin American History," *Latin American Research Review* 17 (3) (1982): 68.
144. There is still a scientific debate on whether the metallurgical amalgamation was discovered in Peru or Europe.
145. John Lynch, "The Institutional Fragments of Colonial Spanish America," *Journal of Latin American Studies* 24 (Quincentenary Supplement) (1992): 78-79. In the eighteenth century, there were fourteen Audiencias in Spanish America.
146. Robert W. Patch, "Imperial Politics and Local Economy in Colonial Central America, 1670-1770," *Past & Present* 143 (May 1994): 77. See also Patch, *Maya and Spaniard in Yucatán, 1648-1812* (Stanford, 1993), 81-90.
147. Christopher Ward, *Imperial Panama: Commerce and Conflict in Isthmian America, 1550-1800* (Albuquerque, N. Mex., 1993), 77-78.
148. William L. Schurz, *The Manila Galleon* (New York, 1959), 365. See also L. A. Clayton, "Trade and Navigation in the Seventeenth-Century Viceroyalty of Peru," *Journal of Latin American Studies* 7 (1) (May 1975): 10.
149. Margarita Suárez, *Comercio y fraude en el Perú colonial*, Serie Estudios Históricos 17 (Lima, 1995), 92-99.
150. Flores Galindo, *Aristocracia y Plebe: Lima, 1760-1830*, 16, 69-77.
151. Jeremy Baskes, "Coerced or Voluntary? The Repartimiento and Market Participation of Peasants in Late Colonial Oaxaca," *Journal of Latin American Studies* 28 (1) (February 1996): 1-28.
152. Juan Marchena Fernández, *Ejército y milicias en el mundo colonial americano* (Madrid, 1992). See also María Gómez Pérez, *El sistema americano: Siglo XVIII* (Madrid, 1992).
153. Scarlett O'Phelan Godoy, *Rebellions and Revolts in Eighteenth Century Peru and Upper Peru* (Cologne, Germany, 1985), 256-73.
154. Elinor C. Burkett, "Indian Women and White Society: The Case of Sixteenth Century Peru," in *Latin American Women: Historical Perspectives*, edited by Asunción Lavrin (Westport, Conn., 1978), 110.
155. Silvio Zavala, *La filosofía política en la conquista de América* (México, D.F., 1993), 38-39.
156. In exchange, Spain received the territory south of the Uruguay River.
157. Mörner, *The Political and Economic Activities of the Jesuits in La Plata Region* (Stockholm, 1953).
158. Pandía Cológeras, *Formacao historica do Brasil* (São Paulo, 1938), 60.
159. Celso Furtado, *Economic Development of Latin America* (London, 1970), 12.
160. Caio Prado, *The Colonial Background of Modern Brazil* (Berkeley, 1967), 133-34.
161. There is not a record of proceedings about the promotion, but beginning in 1720, the king's representative in Brazil had the title of Viceroy.
162. The guarded fleets included about fifty vessels.
163. Contrabandos-Cartas, Informes, 1790, folios 222-26, 328-42, 754-64. See also Mejoras Materiales, Informe, 1770, folios 19-27. Archivo Nacional, Bogotá, Colombia.
164. Nancy M. Farris, *Maya Society under Colonial Rule* (Princeton, 1984), 355-93.
165. Richard Herr, *Rural Changes and Royal Finance in Spain at the End of the Old Regime* (Berkeley, 1986).
166. O. Carlos Stoetzer, *The Scholastic Roots of the Spanish American Revolution* (New York, 1979), 60, 79, 92, 249-63.
167. Vargas Ugarte, *Historia general del Perú*, vol. 6, 352.
168. Timothy E. Anna, *The Fall of the Royal Government in Peru* (Lincoln, Neb., 1979), 214.
169. Patrick Husson, *De la guerra a la rebelión* (Cuzco, 1992), 224, 230-37.

Archives

Contrabandos-Cartas, Informes, 1790, folios 222-26, 328-42, 754-64. Archivo Nacional, Bogotá, Colombia.
Mejoras Materiales, Informe, 1770, folios 19-27. Archivo Nacional, Bogotá.
Real Hacienda (1567-1820), Legajo 125, Expediente 31, folios 1-17. Real Hacienda (1684), Legajo 126, Expediente 54, folios 1-8. Archivo Regional La Libertad, Trujillo, Peru.
Real Hacienda (1786), Causas Ordinarias, Legajo 129, Expediente 110, folios 1-8. Archivo Regional La Libertad, Trujillo.
Ordenanzas del Corregidor de Cajamarca ... para combatir cualquier movimiento de Túpac Amaru, Serie: Corregimiento/Ordinarias, Legajo No. 150, 1781, folios 1-8. Archivo Departamental de Cajamarca, Peru.
Sección Histórica, Legajo 24, Expediente 365, Año 1633, Archivo Departamental de Cajamarca.
Sección Histórica, Serie Corregimiento, Sub-serie: Protección de Naturales, Criminal, Año 1636, Año 1759, Archivo Departamental de Cajamarca.

Interviews

Interview with Dr. Milciades Chávez, professor of Biochemistry, Facultad de Medicina, Universidad Nacional de Trujillo, Peru (July 15, 1978).
Interview with Professor Kobayashi Kazuhiro and Professor Tomohiro Takayama, Sofía University (October 26, 1983, Tokyo, Japan).
Interview with Professor Wu Tai and Professor Chen Kao-hua, History Institute, Peking University (July 10, 1981, Peking, China).
Interview with Professor Tomohiro Takayama, Sofía University (October 26, 1983, Tokyo, Japan).
Interview with the curandero Don Eduardo Calderón Palomino, "El Tuno," (1930-1996), March 4, 1982, Trujillo, Peru.
Interviews on several occasions with the Amazonian curandero Don Elías Avila (1905-1979), Tarapoto, Peru.

Articles, Books, and Other Printed Materials

Abad y Queipo, Manuel. "Estado moral y político en que se hallaba la población del virreynato de la Nueva España en 1799," in *Obras sueltas* by José María Lucio Mora, vol.1. Paris, 1837.
Adams, Richard, ed. *The Origins of Maya Civilization.* Albuquerque, N. Mex., 1977.
Albó, Xavier. "Jesuitas y culturas indígenas," *América Indígena* (México, D.F.) 26 (4)

(1966).

Alcina Franch, José, and Miguel Rivera Dorado. "Exploración arqueológica en la costa de Esmeraldas, Ecuador," *Revista española de antropología americana*, vol. 6 (1971).

Alva Ixtlilxóchitl, Fernando de. *Obras históricas de Don Fernando de Alva Ixtlilxóchitl*, vol. 1. México, D.F., 1965.

Anderson, Robert. "The *Quilombos* of Palmares," *Journal of Latin American Studies* 28 (3) (October 1996).

Andersson, Hans. "One Aspect of Wedin's Work," *The Americas* 25 (2) (October 1968).

Angeles Vargas, Víctor. *Historia del Cuzco*. Lima, 1978.

Anna, Timothy E. *The Fall of the Royal Government in Peru*. Lincoln, Neb., 1979.

Anzoátegui, Ignacio B., ed. *Cristobal Colón: Los cuatro viajes del almirante y su testamento*, Colección Austral. Madrid, 1980.

Arens, William. *The Man-Eating Myth*. Oxford, 1979.

Armillas, Pedro. "The Way to Empire: The Aztec," in *The Indian Background of Latin American History*, edited by Robert Wauchope. New York, 1970.

Arnold, Paul. *El libro maya de los muertos*. México, D.F., 1990.

Atloloni Lecón, Amalia. "El maya, su esclavitud y su comercio," *Memoria del congreso conmemorativo del X aniversario del Departamento de Etnohistoria*, Cuaderno de trabajo No. 4, Instituto nacional de antropología e historia. México, D.F., 1988.

Ayala, Felipe Guamán Poma de. *El primer nueva corónica y buen gobierno*, 3 volumes, edited by John Murra and Rolena Adorno. México, D.F., 1980.

Bartra, Roger. *El modo de producción asiático*. México, D.F., 1969.

Baskes, Jeremy. "Coerced or Voluntary? The *Repartimiento* and Market Participation of Peasants in Late Colonial Oaxaca," *Journal of Latin American Studies* 28 (1) (February 1996).

Batalla Rosado, Juan. "El palacio real mexica," in *Códices, caciques y comunidades*, edited by Maarten Jansen and Luis Reyes García. Leiden, Holland, 1997.

Baudin, Luis. *El imperio socialista de los Incas*. Salta, Argentina, 1970.

Becher, Hans. "Endocanibalismo Yanonámi," *XXXVII Congreso internacional de americanistas: Actas y memorias*, vol. 3. Buenos Aires, 1968.

Bernal, Ignacio. *Mexico Before Cortez: Art, History and Legend*. New York, 1975.

Bishop, Morris. *The Odyssey of Cabeza de Vaca*. New York, 1933.

Boozhong, Song, and Wang Dayaou. "Antiguas relaciones entre China y el Perú," *Debate* (Buenos Aires) 2 (24) (October–November 1994).

Borah, Woodrow. *Early Colonial Trade and Navigation between Mexico and Peru*, Ibero-Americana 38. Berkeley, 1954.

Borah, Woodrow, and Sherburne F. Cook. *The Aboriginal Population of Central Mexico on the Eve of the Spanish Conquest*. Berkeley, 1963.

Bowser, Frederick P. *El esclavo africano en el Perú colonial, 1524–1650*. México, D.F., 1977.

Boxer, C. R. *The Church Militant and Iberian Expansion, 1440–1770*. Baltimore, 1978.

Brand, Donald. *Geographical Explorations by the Spanish and the Portuguese*, The Institute of Latin American Studies of the University of Texas at Austin [1967], 119–120. Offprint Series No. 43.

Braudel, Fernand. *The Wheels of Commerce: Civilization and Capitalism, 15th–18th Century*, 2 volumes. New York, 1979.

Brooks, Francis J. "Motecuzoma Xocoyotl, Hernán Cortés and Bernal Díaz del Castillo:

The Construction of an Arrest," *The Hispanic American Historical Review* 75 (2) (May 1995).

Brundage, Burr C. *Two Earths, Two Heavens: An Essay Contrasting the Aztecs and the Incas.* Albuquerque, N.Mex., 1975.

Burkett, Elinor C. "Indian Women and White Society: The Case of Sixteenth Century Peru," in *Latin American Women: Historical Perspectives,* edited by Asunción Lavrin. Westport, Conn., 1978.

Burland, C. A. *The Gods of Mexico.* New York, 1968.

Burns, E. Bradford. *A History of Brazil.* New York, 1980.

———. *Latin America: A Concise Interpretive History,* 3rd ed. Englewood Cliffs, N.J., 1982.

Burns, Kathryn. "Gender and the Politics of Mestizaje," *The Hispanic American Historical Review* 78 (1) (February 1998).

Burns Glynn, William. "La escritura de los Incas," *Boletín de Lima* 12-14 (May-September 1981).

Cabieses, Fernando. *Dioses y enfermedades: La medicina en el antiguo Perú.* Lima, 1974.

Calnek, Edward E. "Patterns of Empire Formation in the Valley of Mexico," in *The Inca and the Aztec States, 1400-1800,* edited by George A. Collier et al. New York, 1982.

Campbell, Joseph. *Oriental Mythology: The Masks of God.* New York, 1991.

Campbell, Leon G. *The Military and Society in Colonial Peru, 1750-1810.* Philadelphia, 1978.

Carrasco, Pedro. "The Economy of the Aztec and Inca States," in *The Inca and Aztec States, 1400-1800,* edited by George A. Collier et al. New York, 1982.

———. "Some Theoretical Considerations About the Role of the Market in Ancient Mexico," *Economic Anthropology,* edited by Sutti Ortiz. Lanham, Md., 1983.

Céspedes, Guillermo. *Latin America: The Early Years.* New York, 1974.

Chaunu, Pierre. *Historia cuantitativa, historia serial.* México, D.F., 1987.

Cheong, W. E. "Historia de un abandono," *El correo de la UNESCO* (August-September, 1991).

Chevalier, François. *Land and Society in Colonial Mexico: The Great Hacienda.* Berkeley, 1963.

Cieza de León, Pedro. *La primera parte de la chrónica del Perú.* Seville, Spain, 1553.

Clayton, L. A. "Trade and Navigation in the Seventeenth-Century Viceroyalty of Peru," *Journal of Latin American Studies* 7 (1) (May 1975).

Clendinnen, Inga. *Ambivalent Conquests: Maya and Spaniard in Yucatan, 1517-1570.* New York, 1987.

Coe, Michael D. *Breaking the Maya Code.* London, 1992.

Cohen, J. H., ed. *The Discovery and Conquest of Peru.* Baltimore, 1968.

Cológeras, Pandía. *Formaçao historica do Brasil.* São Paulo, 1938.

Colón, Cristobal. *Diario de navegación y otros escritos,* Biblioteca de clásicos dominicanos. Santo Domingo, 1988.

Contreras, Carlos. *Los Mineros y el Rey, los Andes del Norte: Hualgayoc 1770-1825,* Serie Estudios Históricos 16. Lima, 1995.

Cook, Noble D. *Demographic Collapse: Indian Peru, 1520-1620.* Cambridge, U.K., 1981.

Cortés, Hernán. *Cartas de relación de la conquista de México,* 6th ed., Colección Austral. Madrid, 1979.

Crosby, Alfred W. *The Columbian Exchange.* Westport, Conn., 1976.

————. *Ecological Imperialism*. Cambridge, U.K., 1993.

D'Altroy, Terrence N. *Provincial Power in the Inka Empire*. Washington, D.C., 1992.

Díaz, Bernal. *The Conquest of New Spain*, translated by J. H. Cohen. Baltimore, 1967.

Díaz del Castillo, Bernal. *The True History of the Conquest of Mexico*. La Jolla, Calif., 1979.

Díaz Infante, Fernando. *La educación de los Aztecas*. México, D.F., 1988.

Dobyns, Henry. "Estimating Aboriginal American Population: An Appraisal of Techniques with a New Hemispheric Estimate," *Current Anthropology* 7 (1966).

————. "An Outline of Andean Epidemic History to 1720," *Bulletin of the History of Medicine* 37 (6) (1963).

Dreyfus, Simone. "Historical and Political Inter-Connections," in "Themes in Political Organization: The Caribs and Their Neighbors," edited by Audrey B. Colson and H. Dieter Heinen, *Antropológica* (Caracas, 1983-1984).

El Comercio (Lima), July 1, 1978.

El Comercio (Lima), July 12, 1978.

Eriksson, Olof. *Autoteleteknik*, 3rd ed. Stockholm, 1969.

Espinoza Soriano, Waldemar. *La destrucción del imperio de los Incas*. Lima, 1977.

Fakta (Oslo), May 1988.

Farriss, Nancy M. *Maya Society under Colonial Rule*. Princeton, 1984.

Fernández de Oviedo y Valdés, Gonzalo. *Natural History of the West Indies*. Translated and edited by Sterling Stoudemire. Chapel Hill, N.C., 1959.

Flores Galindo, Alberto. *Aristocracia y plebe: Lima, 1760-1830*. Lima, 1984.

————. *Buscando un Inca: Identidad y utopía en los Andes*. Havana, 1986.

Florescano, Enrique. "Una nueva Historia de los Mayas," *América Indígena* (México, D.F.), 50 (1) (January–March 1990).

Floyd, Troy S., ed. *The Bourbon Reformers and Spanish Civilization*. Boston, 1966.

Forbes, Jack D. *Apache, Navaho and Spaniard*. Norman, Okla., 1994.

Frank, E. "Stone Working in Ancient Peru," *Archaeometry* 22 (2) (1980).

Friede, Juan. "Origenes de la esclavitud indígena en Venezuela," *América Indígena* 22 (1) (1962).

Friede, Juan, and Benjamin Keen, eds. *Bartolomé de Las Casas in History*. DeKalb, Ill., 1971.

Fuente, Beatriz de la. *Los hombres de piedra: Escultura Olmeca*. México, D.F., 1977.

Furtado, Celso. *Economic Development of Latin America*. London, 1970.

Gagliano, Joseph A. *Coca Prohibition in Peru: The Historical Debates*. Tucson, Ariz., 1994.

García Soriano, Manuel. *El conquistador español del siglo XVI*. Tucumán, Argentina, 1954.

Garcilaso de la Vega, Inca. *Comentarios reales de los Incas*, 3 volumes. Lima, 1973.

Garibay, Angel María, ed. *Vida económica de Tenochtitlán*. México, D.F., 1961.

Georgescu-Roegen, Nicholas. *Energy and Economic Myths: Institutional and Analytical Economic Essays*. New York, 1976.

Gibson, Charles. "The Aztec Aristocracy in Colonial Mexico," *Comparative Studies in Society and History*, vol. 2 (1959-1960).

————. *The Aztecs under Spanish Rule*. Stanford, 1964.

————, ed. *The Spanish Tradition in America*. New York, 1968.

————. *Tlaxcala in the Sixteenth Century*, 2nd ed. Stanford, 1967.

Gillespie, Susan D. *The Aztec Kings: The Construction of Rulership in Mexican History*. Tucson, Ariz., 1989.

Gómez Pérez, María. *El sistema americano: Siglo XVIII*. Madrid, 1992.

Góngora, Mario. *Studies in Colonial History of Spanish America*. London, 1975.

Gordon, Cyrus. *Before Columbus*. London, 1971.

Greenleaf, Richard E. *Zumarraga and the Mexican Inquisition, 1536-1543*. Washington, D.C., 1962.

Guillén, Edmundo. *Versión inca de la conquista*. Lima, 1974.

Gunn, Joel, and Richard Adams. "Climatic Change, Culture and Civilization in North America," *World Archaeology* 13 (1) (June 1981).

Haas, Jonathan. *The Evolution of the Prehistoric State*. New York, 1982.

Hamond, Norman, and Gordon P. Willey. *Maya Archeology and Ethno-History*. Austin, Tex., 1979.

Hanke, Lewis U. *Aristotle and the American Indians: A Study of Race Prejudice in the Modern World*. London, 1959.

Hardoy, Jorge E. *Pre-Columbian Cities*. London, 1973.

Harris, Marvin. *Cows, Pigs, Wars and Witches*. New York, 1974.

Harth-Terre, Emilio, and Alberto Márquez Abanto. "El histórico puente sobre el río Apurimac," *Revista del archivo nacional del Perú* 25 (1961).

Harvey, H.R., and B.J. Williams. "Aztec Arithmetic: Positional Notation and Area Calculation," *Science* 210 (31) (October 1980).

Hassig, Ross. *Mexico and the Spanish Conquest*. London, 1994.

Heiser, Charles B. *Seed to Civilization*. San Francisco, 1973.

Helms, Mary W. *Ancient Panama: Chiefs in Search of Power*. Austin, Tex., 1979.

———. *Middle America*. Englewood Cliffs, N.J., 1975.

Hemming, John. *The Conquest of the Incas*. New York, 1970.

Herr, Richard. *Rural Changes and Royal Finance in Spain at the End of the Old Regime*. Berkeley, 1986.

Heyerdahl, Thor. *Early Man and the Ocean*. Garden City, N.Y., 1979.

———. *Sjövägarna till Polynesien*. Stockholm, 1967.

Hopkins, David M., ed. *The Bering Land Bridge*. Stanford, 1967.

Horna, Hernán. "A propósito del descubrimiento asiático de América," *América Indígena* (México, D.F.), 52 (1-2) (January–June 1992).

Hume, Peter, and Neil L. Whitehead. *Wild Majesty Encounters with Caribs from Columbus to the Present Day*. Oxford, 1992.

Husson, Patrick. *De la guerra a la rebelión*. Cuzco, 1992.

Hyslop, John. *The Inka Road System*. Orlando, Fla., 1984.

Ingstad, Helge. "Norse Explorers and Norse Sites at L'Anse Aux Meadows," in *The Quest for America*, edited by Geoffrey Ashe et al. New York, 1971.

Izumi, Seiichi, and Kazuo Terada. *Excavations at Kotosh, Peru*. Tokyo, 1972.

Jansen, Maarten. "La serpiente emplumada y el amanecer de la historia," in *Códices, caciques y comunidades*, edited by Maarten Jansen and Luis Reyes García. Leiden, Holland, 1997.

Jara, Victoria de la. *Introducción al estudio de la escritura de los Inkas*. Lima, 1975.

Juan, Jorge, and Antonio de Ulloa. *A Voyage to South America*. New York, 1964.

Katz, Friedrich. *Ancient American Civilizations*. New York, 1972.

Kauffman Doig, Federico. *Manual de arqueología peruana*. Lima, 1980.

Keith, Donald H., and Christian J. Buys. "New Light on Medieval Chinese Seagoing Ship Construction," *The International Journal of Nautical Archeology* 10 (2) (May 1981).

Keith, Robert G. *Conquest and Agrarian Change: The Emergence of the Hacienda System on the Peruvian Coast*. Cambridge, Mass., 1976.

———, ed. *Haciendas and Plantations in Latin American History*. New York, 1977.

Kidder II, Alfred. "South American Penetrations in Middle America," in *The Maya and Their Neighbors*, edited by Clarence L. Hay et al. New York, 1977.

Klor de Alva, J. Jorge. "Martín Ocelotl," in *Struggle and Survival*, edited by David Sweet and Gary Nash. Berkeley, 1981.

Knórozov, Y. V. *Códices jeroglíficos de los Mayas*. Leningrad, 1975.

Kobayashi, Munehiro. *Tres estudios sobre el sistema tributario de los Mexicas*. México, D.F., 1993.

La Prensa (Lima), July 8, 1978.

"La trepanación peruana se difundió en Centroamérica," *El Comercio* (Lima), February 17, 1982.

Ladd, Doris M. *The Mexican Nobility at Independence, 1780–1826*. Austin, Tex., 1976.

Lafaye, Jacques. *Quetzalcóatl and Guadalupe: The Formation of Mexican National Consciousness, 1531–1813*, translated by Benjamin Keen. Chicago, 1979.

Landa, Diego de. *Relación de las cosas de Yucatán*, edited by A. M. Tozzer. Cambridge, Mass., 1941.

Larco Hoyle, Rafael. "La escritura mochica sobre pallares," *Revista geográfica americana* (Buenos Aires) 18 (107) (August 1942).

———. *Los mochicas*, 2 volumes. Lima, 1939.

Las Casas, Bartolomé de. *History of the Indies*, edited by Andrew Collard. New York, 1971.

———. "A Very Brief Relation of the Destruction of the Indians, 1552," in *The Black Legend*, edited by Charles Gibson. New York, 1969.

Lechtman, Heather. "Pre-Columbian Surface Metallurgy," *Scientific American* 250 (June 1984).

León-Portilla, Miguel. *Los antiguos mexicanos a través de sus crónicas y cantares*. México, D.F., 1961.

———. *De besegrades version*. Stockholm, 1971.

———. *Pre-Columbian Literature of Mexico*. Norman, Okla., 1969.

———. "¿Qué es el indigenismo interamericano?," *América Indígena* 26 (4) (1966).

Lettner, Carlos J. "Las escrituras americanas," *Anuario Indigenista* 33 (December 1973).

Levathes, Louise. *When China Ruled the Seas*. New York, 1994.

Li, Dun J. *The Ageless Chinese*. New York, 1965.

Lizárraga, Reginaldo de. *Descripción breve de toda la tierra del Perú, Tucumán, Río de la Plata y Chile*, Nueva biblioteca de autores españoles, vol. 15. Madrid, 1909.

Llosa Porras, Fernando. *Sechín: Monumento-Mito*. Lima, 1999.

Lockhart, James. *The Men of Cajamarca: A Social and Biographical Study of the First Conquerors of Peru*. Austin, Tex., 1972.

Lockhart, James, and Enrique Otte, eds. *Letters and People of the Spanish Indies: The Sixteenth Century*. London, 1976.

López de Gómara, Francisco. *Cortés: The Life of the Conqueror by His Secretary*, translated by Lesley Bird Simpson. Berkeley, 1966.

Lothrop, Samuel K. "Peruvian Stylistic Impact on Lower Central America," in *Essays in Pre-Columbian Art and Arqueology*, edited by Lothrop et al. Cambridge, Mass., 1961.

Lou, Dennis. "Chinese Inscriptions Found in Pre-Columbian Objects," *XXXVII Congreso internacional de americanistas: Actas y memorias*, vol. 4. Buenos Aires, 1968.

———. "The Mesoamerican "Mushroom Stones' and the Chinese Ancestor Tablets,"

XXXVI Congreso internacional de americanistas: Actas y memorias, vol. 1. Madrid, 1964.

Lovell, W. George. *Conquest and Survival in Colonial Guatemala*. Montreal, 1985.

Lumbreras, Luis G. *La arqueología como ciencia social*. Lima, 1974.

Luxemburg, Rosa. *Introducción a la economía*. Madrid, 1974.

Lynch, John. "The Institutional Fragments of Colonial Spanish America," *Journal of Latin American Studies* 24 (Quincentenary Supplement) (1992).

Macera, Pablo. *Historia del Perú: La colonia*, 3 volumes. Lima, 1985.

Macleod, Murdo J. *Spanish Central America*. Berkeley, 1973.

Major, R. H., ed. *Christopher Columbus: Four Voyages to the New World, Letters and Selected Documents*. New York, 1961.

Marchant, Alexander. *From Barter to Slavery*. Baltimore, 1941.

Marchena Fernández, Juan. *Ejército y milicias en el mundo colonial americano*. Madrid, 1992.

Marcos, Jorge. "De ida y vuelta a Acapulco con mercaderes de mullu," in *Arqueología de la costa ecuatoriana*, edited by Jorge Marcos. Quito, 1986.

Marcus, Joyce. "Zapotec Writing," *Scientific American* 242 (February 1980).

Martinsson-Wallin, Helene. *Ahu—The Ceremonial Stone Structures of Easter Island*, Societas Archaeologica Upsaliensis, Aun 19. Uppsala, 1994.

Mason, J. Alden. *The Ancient Civilizations of Peru*. New York, 1971.

Matos Mar, José. *Yanaconaje y reforma agraria en el Perú*. Lima, 1976.

Matos Mendieta, Ramiro. "El secreto de la Quilca," *El Comercio* (Lima), November 24, 1985.

Meggers, Betty J. "Contacts from Asia," in *The Quest for America*, edited by Geoffrey Ashe et al. New York, 1971.

———. "The Transpacific Origin of Mesoamerican Civilization," *American Anthropologist* 77 (1) (March 1975).

Meggers, Betty J., Clifford Evans, and Emilio Estrada. *Early Formative Period of Coastal Ecuador: The Valdivia and Machialilla Phases*. Washington, D.C., 1965.

Melville, Elinor G. K. *A Plague of Sheep: Enviromental Consequences of the Conquest of Mexico*. New York, 1994.

Mendes Correa, A. A. "O signifcado genealógico do 'australopithecus' e do cranio de tabgha e o arco antropofilético índico," *Trabalhos sociales portugueses antropológicos* 2 (3) (1925).

Montesinos, Fernando de. *Memorias antiguas e historiales del Perú*, edited by Phillip A. Means. London, 1920.

Morison, Samuel Eliot, ed. *Journals and Other Documents on the Life and Voyages of Christopher Columbus*. New York, 1963.

Mörner, Magnus. *The Andean Past: Land, Societies and Conflicts*. New York, 1985.

———. *La corona española y los foráneos en los pueblos de indios de América*. Estocolmo, 1970.

———. *The Political and Economic Activities of the Jesuits in the La Plata Region: The Habsburg Era*. Stockholm, 1953.

———. *Race Mixture in the History of Latin America*. Boston, 1967.

———. "Wedin's Work in General," *The Americas* 25 (2) (October 1968).

Mörner, Magnus, et al. "Comparative Approaches to Latin American History," *Latin American Research Review* 17 (3) (1982).

Murra, John. *Formaciones económicas y políticas en el mundo andino*. Lima, 1975.

———. *La organización económica del Estado inca*. México, D.F., 1989.

Murúa, Martín de. *Historia general del Perú y descendencia de los incas*, edited by

Manuel Ballesteros Gaibrois, 2 volumes. Madrid, 1962.

Narby, Jeremy. *La serpiente cósmica: El ADN y los orígenes del saber.* Lima, 1997.

Needham, Joseph. *Clerks and Craftsmen in China and the West.* Cambridge, U.K., 1970.

Nordenskiöld, Erland. "The Secrets of the Peruvian Quipus," *Comparative Ethnological Studies* (Gothenburg), vol. 6 (1925).

O'Brien, Patrick. "European Economic Development: The Contribution of the Periphery," *The Economic History Review* 35 (1) (February 1982).

O'Phelan Godoy, Scarlett. *Rebellions and Revolts in Eighteenth Century Peru and Upper Peru.* Cologne, Germany, 1985.

Over, Raymond Van, ed. *I Ching.* New York, 1971.

Pacey, Arnold. *Technology in World Civilization, a Thousand-Year History.* Cambridge, Mass., 1990.

Padden, R. C. *The Hummingbird and the Hawk.* New York, 1967.

Patch, Robert W. "Imperial Politics and Local Economy in Colonial Central America, 1670-1770," *Past & Present* 143 (May 1994).

———. *Maya and Spaniard in Yucatán, 1648-1812.* Stanford, 1993.

Pease G., Franklin. *Del Tawantinsuyo a la historia del Perú.* Lima, 1978.

Peterson, Frederick. *Ancient Mexico.* New York, 1962.

Piel, Jean. *Capitalisme agraire au Pérou.* Paris, 1975.

Pizarro, Pedro. *Relación del descubrimiento y conquista de los reinos del Perú,* Biblioteca de Autores Españoles, 168. Madrid, 1965.

Popol Vuh, edited by Adrián Recinos. México D.F., 1994.

Poppino, Rollie E. *Brazil: The Land and People.* New York, 1968.

Porras Barrenechea, Raúl. *Fuentes históricas peruanas.* Lima, 1945.

———, ed. *Relación del descubrimiento del reyno del Perú que hizo Diego de Trujillo.* Seville, Spain, 1948.

Prado, Caio. *The Colonial Background of Modern Brazil.* Berkeley, 1967.

Quimby, George I. "Culture Contact on the Northwest Coast, 1785-1795," *American Anthropologist* 50 (2) (June 1948).

Quinn, David B., ed. *New American World: A Documentary History of North America to 1612,* 5 volumes. New York, 1979.

Rivet, Paul. *Les origins de l'homme americain.* Paris, 1957.

Ronan, Colin A. *The Cambridge Illustrated History of the World's Science.* London, 1983.

Rosenblat, Angel. *La población indígena de América desde 1492 hasta la actualidad.* Buenos Aires, 1945.

Rostworowski, María. *Doña Francisca Pizarro.* Lima, 1989.

———. *Ensayos de historia andina.* Lima, 1993.

———. *La mujer en el Perú precolombino,* Documento de trabajo No. 72. Lima, 1995.

———. *Pachacamac y el señor de los milagros: Una trayectoria milenaria.* Lima, 1992.

Rounds, J. "Dynastic Succession and the Centralization of Power in Tenochtitlán," in *The Inca and Aztec States, 1400-1800,* edited by George A. Collier et al. New York, 1982.

Rouse, Irving. *The Tainos.* New Haven and London, 1992.

Rowe, John. "Absolute Chronology in the Andean Area," *American Antiquity* 10 (3) (1945).

———. "Inca Culture at the Time of the Spanish Conquest," in *Handbook of South*

American Indians, vol. 2, edited by Julian Steward. Washington, D.C., 1946.

Sáamanos, Juan de. *Relación de los primeros descubrimientos de Francisco Pizarro y Diego de Almagro*, Colección de documentos inéditos para la historia de España, vol. 5. Madrid, 1844.

Saffer, Lynda. *Native Americans Before 1492*. New York, 1992.

Salles-Reese, Verónica. "Las divergencias semióticas y el proceso de mestizaje en el Perú colonial," *Colonial Latin American Review* 5 (1) (June 1996).

Sallnow, Michael J. *Pilgrims of the Andes: Regional Cults in Cuzco*. Washington, D.C., 1987.

Salomon, Frank. "A North Andean Trader Complex under Inca Rule," *Ethnohistory* 34 (2) (1987).

Sánchez-Albornoz, Nicolás. *La población de América Latina desde los tiempos precolombinos hasta el año 2000*. Madrid, 1977.

———. *The Population of Latin America: A History*. Berkeley, 1974.

Sarmiento de Gamboa, Pedro. *History of the Incas*. Cambridge, U.K., 1907.

Sauer, Carl O. *The Early Spanish Main*. Berkeley, 1966.

Scarbough, Vernon L., and Gary G. Gallopin. "A Water Storage in the Maya Lowlands," *Science* 251 (4994) (February 1991).

Scarón, Pedro, ed. *Karl Marx, Friedrich Engels: Materiales para la historia de América Latina*. México, D.F., 1975.

Schele, Linda, and David Freidel. *A Forest of Kings: The Untold Story of the Ancient Maya*. New York, 1990.

Schurz, William L. *The Manila Galleon*. New York, 1959.

Schwartz, Stuart B. *Sovereignty and Society in Colonial Brazil*. Berkeley, 1973.

Seed, Patricia. "'Are These Not Also Men?': The Indians' Humanity for Spanish Civilization," *Journal of Latin American Studies* 25 (3) (October 1993).

Sempat Assadourian, Carlos. "The Colonial Economy: The Transfer of the European System of Production," *Journal of Latin American Studies* 24 (Quincentenary Supplement) (1992).

Shao, Paul. *Asiatic Influences in Pre-Columbian Art*. Ames, Iowa, 1976.

———. *The Origin of Ancient American Cultures*. Ames, Iowa, 1983.

Sharer, Robert. "The Maya Collapse Revisited: Internal and External Perspectives," in *Social Process in Maya Prehistory*, edited by Norman Hamond. Baltimore, 1977.

Shimada, Izumi, and John F. Merkel. "Copper-Alloy Metallurgy in Ancient Peru," *Scientific American* 264 (July 1991).

Silva Santisteban, Fernando. *Los obrajes en el virreynato del Perú*. Lima, 1964.

Silverblatt, Irene. *Moon, Sun, and Witches*. Princeton, 1987.

Silverman, Gail. *El tejido andino: Un libro de sabiduría*. Lima, 1994.

Slicher Van Bath, B. H. *Real hacienda y economía en Hispanoamérica, 1541–1820*. Amsterdam, 1989.

Smith, Michael E. "Life in the Provinces of the Aztec Empire," *Scientific American* 270 (September 1997).

Stark, Louise. "Maya-Yunga-Chipayan: A New Linguistic Alignment," *International Journal of American Linguistics* 37 (2) (1972).

Stavrianos, L. S. *The World to 1500*. Englewood Cliffs, N.J., 1982.

Stein, Stanley J., and Barbara H. Stein. *The Colonial Heritage of Latin America*. New York, 1970.

Stern, Steve J. *Peru's Indian Peoples and the Challenge of the Spanish Conquest: Huamanga to 1640*. Madison, Wis., 1982.

———, ed. *Resistance, Rebellion and Consciousness in the Andean Peasant World*,

18th to 20th Centuries. Madison, Wis., 1987.

———. "The Rise and Fall of Indian and White Alliances," *The Hispanic American Historical Review* 61 (3) (August 1981).

Stewart, T. D. *The People of America.* New York, 1973.

Stoetzer, O. Carlos. *The Scholastic Roots of the Spanish American Revolution.* New York, 1979.

Stuart, David, and Stephen D. Houston. "Maya Writing," *Scientific American* 261 (August 1989).

Suárez, Margarita. *Comercio y fraude en el Perú colonial,* Serie Estudios Históricos 17. Lima, 1995.

Tapia, Andrés de. "Relación sobre la conquista de México," in *Colección de documentos para la historia de México,* edited by Joaquín García Icazbalceta, 5 volumes. México, 1866.

Taylor, William B. *Drinking, Homicide, and Rebellion in Colonial Mexican Villages.* Stanford, 1979.

Tello, Julio C. *Las edades en el Perú por Guamán Poma,* Museo de Antropología. Lima, 1939.

———. *Wira-Kocha.* Lima, 1923.

Thevet, André. "La cosmographie universelle," in *Les français en Amérique pendant la deuxième moité de XVIe siècle: le Brésil et les bresiliens,* edited by Suzanne Lussagnet. Paris, 1953.

Tibesar, Antonine. *Franciscan Beginnings in Colonial Peru.* Washington, D.C., 1953.

"Till sjös och på land," *Kina rapport* 3. Stockholm, 1980.

Todorov, Tzvetan. *The Conquest of America.* New York, 1985.

"Torka utrotade mayafolket," *Illustrated Vetenskap* 13 (December 1996).

Tovar, Hermes. *Notas sobre el modo de producción precolombino.* Bogotá, 1974.

Tozzer, Alfred M. "Landa's Relation de las Cosas de Yucatán," *Papers of the Peabody Museum of American Arqueology and Ethnology,* vol. 18. Cambridge, Mass., 1941.

Vargas Ugarte, Rubén, S. J. *Historia general del Perú: Virreynato,* 6 volumes. Lima, 1971.

Vega, Juan José. *La guerra de los viracochas,* Colección Biblioteca Peruana. Lima, 1963.

Verrill, A. Hyatt, and Ruth Verrill. *America's Ancient Civilizations.* New York, 1967.

Wallerstein, Immanuel. *The Modern World-System II: Mercantilism and the Consolidation of the European World Economy.* New York, 1980.

Ward, Christopher. *Imperial Panama: Commerce and Conflict in Isthmian America, 1550-1800.* Albuquerque, N. Mex., 1993.

Wauchope, Robert. "Late Horizonts of Maya Prehistory," in *The Indian Background of Latin American History,* edited by Wauchope. New York, 1970.

Wedin, Åke. *El concepto de lo incaico.* Uppsala, Sweden, 1966.

———. *La cronología de la historia incaica: Estudio crítico.* Madrid, 1963.

Wolfe, Eric R. *Europe and the People Without History.* Berkeley, 1997.

Zantwijk, Rudolf van. "El origen de la sociedad y el estado aztecas así como la historicidad de las fuentes autóctonas, una introducción," *Boletín de estudios latinoamericanos y del Caribe* (Amsterdam) 18 (June 1975).

Zavala, Silvio. *La filosofía política en la conquista de América.* México, D.F., 1993.

Zubriski, Yu. *Los incas quechuas.* Moscú, 1979.

Zuidema, R. Tom. *Inca Civilization in Cuzco.* Austin, Tex., 1990.

Abad y Queipo, Manuel 95
Agriculture 11-14, 39, 43, 49-50, 62, 72, 81, 111, 141, 146
Aldana, Lorenzo de 99
Aldeias 116-17
Aleutian Islands 21
Anakaona 82
Anthropophagy 86
Apoxpalón 108
Arawak 81, 83
Arens, William 86
Arias Dávila, Pedro 97
Arnold, Paul 37
Atahualpa 73, 75, 90, 92-93, 97-102, 124, 128
Ayllu 64
Aztecs 34-37, 39, 46-51, 53, 56, 66, 87, 90-91, 95, 101-102, 105, 107-108, 128
Aztlán 49

Bandeirantes 116, 144
Barthel, Thomas 76-77
Behecchio 82
Bourbon Reforms 114, 133, 136, 139, 142
Bourbons 121, 137-39, 147
Brundage, Burr C. 51
Burns, E. Bradford 61

Cabildos 137
Cacamatzin 91
Caciques 81, 85, 96, 119, 128, 130-32, 135, 138-39, 148
Cadiz 114, 150
Cajamarca x, 97-99, 101, 131
Calendar 39, 41, 62, 71, 103
Calpulli 50
Cañaris 102-103
Canibas 82-86
Caonabó 82, 84-85, 93
Careta 96
Cartagena 114
Castilla del Oro 88
Cayuchi, Ninan 97-98

Céspedes, Guillermo 13
Chachapuyas 102
Chan Chan 17-19, 21
Chan, Hui 21
Chang Dynasty 17
Chavín 17, 46, 57
Chectemal 88, 94
Chichén Itzá 39, 44, 48
Chima 96
China x, 4, 13, 17-22, 24, 26, 28, 37, 62, 72, 113
Chincha 57, 63, 101, 107
Cieza de León, Pedro 75
Clendinnen, Inga 33
Columbus, Christopher 3, 28, 81
Comagre 96
Constitution of 1812 150
Consulado 114, 136
Cook, Noble 57
Copán 39
Corregidores 119, 121, 137-39
Cortés, Hernán 34, 73, 85-86
Costner, Kevin 7
Cozumel 87-88
Criollos 5, 95, 114, 124, 126-28, 131-35, 137, 139, 148-50
Cuatequil 50, 120, 134
Cuauhtémoc 108
Cult of death 65
Cult of the dragon 18

De Aguilar, Jerónimo 88, 90
De Landa, Diego 31, 94
Díaz del Castillo, Bernal 19, 73, 87
Diffusionism 29-30
Discrimination 3, 7
Dobyns, Henry 57

Easter Island 20, 28
Encomienda 118-20, 123, 140-42
Ethnohistory ix, 3

Felipillo 96, 101, 107

Flores Galindo, Alberto 132
Florescano, Enrique 36
Fusang 21, 26

Galindo, César 7
García Hurtado, Federico 7
Garcia, Aleixo 98
Garcilaso de la Vega, Inca 131
Gibson, Charles 6, 50
Grijalva, Juan de 88
Grotius, Hugo 24
Guacanagarí 82, 84, 93
Guerrero, Gonzalo 88, 90

Hassig, Ross 91
Hatuey 106
Heizer, Robert 22
Heyerdahl, Thor 69
Hoffman, Dustin 6
Huaka Tanka 33
Huancas 102
Huari 57
Huascar 98
Humboldt, Alexander von 75, 111, 130
Hyslop, John 68

I-Ching 43
Inca, Manco 92, 102-103
Indianos 114, 134, 136, 150
Indigenista 6
Indios Principales 127
Intiwatana 71

Japan x, 4, 21-22, 26, 52
Jara, Victoria de la 76-77
Jesuits 116-17, 122, 140, 144-45
Julianillo 87
Just wars 117

Knórozov, Yuri V. 37
Kon-Tiki 69
Kukul-Chan 19, 48

Larco Hoyle, Rafael 76
Laws of Burgos 140
Liberalism 5, 149
Liberals 150
Linneus 24
Luxemburg, Rosa 59

Macegual 50, 54
Macera, Pablo 90
Mamelucos 115-16
Manila 112-13
Martinillo 96-97, 101, 107
Marx, Karl 59, 109
Mathematics 50
Mayeque 50, 133
Medicine 70-71
Meggers, Betty J. 22
Melchorejo 87
Mendes Correa, A. A. 8
Menéndez Pidal, Ramón 31
Mesoamerica 4, 12-13, 17, 21, 23, 33, 36, 39,
   45, 47, 50, 56, 62-63, 65, 71, 106-108,
   123
Metallurgy 48, 69
Migration(s) x, 4, 8-9, 46-47, 82
Ming Dynasty 22
Minka 64
Minorities, ethnic 3
Missions 116, 140, 143-45
Mississippi culture 14
Mita 64, 107, 120-23, 134
Mitayos 120-23, 134, 138
Mochicas 17
Molina, Alonso de 96
Monte Albán 47
Montezuma 73, 87, 89-93, 99-100, 102,
   127-28
Mörner, Magnus 56
Muenala, Alberto 7
Murra, John 65

Naborias 81
Narby, Jeremy 71
New Laws (1542) 141
Nitaínos 81
Nordenskiöld, Erland 72
Núñez de Balboa, Vasco 20, 96

O'Brien, Patrick 109
Obrajes 121-22, 130, 138
Ocllo, Cura 102
Olmecs 37, 39, 46, 57
Ortega, Juan 90

Padden, R.C. 19, 34
Palenque 39
Palmares 116

Panacas 64
Panama 20, 40, 68, 88, 96, 107–108
Panquiaco 96
Patronato 137
Pax Aztecana 51
Pax Teotihuacana 47
Petén 39
Peterson, Frederick 30
Pinzón, Martín Alonzo de 82
Pizarro, Francisco 73, 89, 96, 99, 101, 128
Pizarro, Hernando 92, 128
Pizarro, Pedro 101
Plagues, European 57, 91
Polo, Marco 15
Polynesia 20, 69, 85
Popol Vuh 33
Portobelo 114
Potosí 118, 121
Prado, Caio 146
Pumacahua, Mateo 132

Quetzalcoatl 19, 48
Quigaltan 93
Quilcas 56, 75–76
Quilombos 116
Quipus 72, 74–76

Racism 5, 31
Radicati, Carlos 76
Reductions 117, 124, 129, 134, 144
Religious fanaticism 31, 33
Repartimiento 118–23, 127–28, 134
Reparto comercial 138–39
Republic of Spaniards 126, 131
Republic of the Indians 133
Requerimiento 87, 99
Rig Veda 19
Rouse, Irving 83
Rowe, John 56
Royal Fifth 111

Sacrifice, human 33–35, 47–48
Sanjinés, Jorge 7
Santos Atahualpa, Juan 124
Scandinavians x, 17
Schele, Linda 37
Science fiction 24
Señor de los Milagros 94
Seville 113–14, 136, 140, 150
Silva Santisteban, Fernando 122

Silverman, Gail 76
Smith, Adam 109
Smith, Joseph 24
Social Darwinism 5
Soto, Hernando de 92–93, 99
Subdelegates 139

Taino 82, 84, 86, 106
Tajín 47
Tawantinsuyo 57, 59, 61, 65, 98, 102, 107
Tenochtitlán 48–49, 89–90, 95
Teotihuacán 40, 47
Texcoco 46–48
Thompson, Eric 39, 44
Tiahuanaco 57
Tikal 39, 43
Tlatoque 54
Todorov, Tzvetan 12
Toledo, Francisco de 73
Toltecs 37, 39, 44, 47–48, 57
Tonantzin 94
Torquemada, Juan de 23
Tovar Pinzón, Hermes 65
Tula 47–48

Valdivia 23
Valera, Blas de 96
Valverde, Vicente de 99
Vilcabamba 103
Viracocha 19
Virgin of Guadalupe 94

Wachtel, Nathan 80
Wedin, Åke 56
Writing, Incan 75–77
Writing, Mayan 37–38

Xochicalco 47

Yanaconas 65–66, 134
Yong-le 22
Yoruba 95
Yupanqui, Dionisio 130–31

Zemis 81
Zumárraga, Juan de 34
Zurita, Felix 6